CHUCK
AMUCK

THE LIFE AND TIMES OF AN ANIMATED CARTOONIST

CHUCK AMUCK

by CHUCK JONES

FOREWORD BY STEVEN SPIELBERG

AVON BOOKS ◆ NEW YORK

All events related in this volume are either real or fictional—the drawings have been changed to protect the innocent.

SGT. JOE MONDAY   DETECTIVE SHMOE TUESDAY

From ROCKET SQUAD *(1956)*

☐

The Farrar, Straus and Giroux edition contains the following Library of Congress Cataloging in Publication Data:
Jones, Chuck.
Chuck amuck: the life and times of an animated cartoonist / Chuck Jones ; with a foreword by Steven Spielberg.
p.   cm.
1. Jones, Chuck.   2. Animators—United States— Biography.   I. Title.
NC1766.U52J66   1989   741.5'8'092—dc20   [B]   89-1444

First Avon Books Trade Printing: November 1990

I dedicate this book to my wife, Marian,
and to my daughter, Linda,
who together through light touch,
light heart, and deep love have
made these past years the happiest,
the best years of a happy life.

(Je vous embrasse tendrement.)

☐

. . . and to Stefan Kanfer,
whose determination that there was a book lurking
in the shadows of my shadowy history put me,
because of my love for him,
into the uneasy position of having
to try to prove him right.

☐

But without Linda Healey: superb editor,
enemy of the false,
friend of the true,
even this wan hope would have been only fantasy.

C O N T

E N T S

F   O   R   E

When you hear the name Chuck Jones, what is the first image that comes to mind?

For me, that generically American-sounding name always had the familiar ring of the family next door. One feels compelled to trust a name like that. It's the type of person you might take a broken baseball bat to when your own dad is too busy to glue it . . . It's the local Scoutmaster . . . the greengrocer . . . the best auto mechanic in town.

It's not the sort of name one instantly associates with pesky wabbits, neurotic ducks, or hard-luck coyotes, is it?

Doorlock Homes
pursues his prey

W O R D

If Walt Disney was the first animator who taught me how to fly in my dreams, Chuck Jones was the first animator who made me laugh at them.

With the creation of Pepé Le Pew, Coyote, and Road Runner, and as part of the team that created Daffy Duck, Porky Pig, and directed over fifty Bugs Bunny cartoons, Chuck broke away from the sweet preschool characters to whom Walt Disney Productions had given eternal life.

Birdus Fleetus and Lupus Persisticus were my childhood heroes. It was out of a heartfelt respect for his cartoon wizardry that I begged Universal to pay Warners for those forty composite seconds of film that lent my first film, *The Sugarland Express*, its most poignant moment.

Knowing Chuck has been a treat and I thank him for teaching me so much about breaking all the laws of physics . . . just for the joy of it.

Voilà!

Steven Spielberg

C A V E A T

An autobiography that leaves out little things and enumerates only the big ones is no proper picture of the man's life at all; his life consists of his feelings and his interests, with here and there an incident apparently big or little to hang the feelings on.

— MARK TWAIN

This book is not a record of facts, it is not exact; it makes no claim to being exact; it is, I hope, a fond catchall, a remembrance of events and people who, consciously or not, shaped my life and character.

All memories are faulty, of course, and some autobiographies are bitter or rueful and waste valuable time seeking to identify those people who were, in the narrator's memory, responsible for many of his stumblings and failures.

This book has no one to blame and very many to praise and to love. Like my contemporaries Wile E. Coyote and Daffy Duck, I have little time and no inclination to find fault or failure in others, for I have too many abundant and stimulating faults and failures of my very own. Recognition of my own ineptitudes has always led me to better understanding of my trade. Jumblings, mistakes, and errors in judgment are the essence, the very fabric of humor.

Dr. Watkins

E M P T O R

While I have not attempted a thorough and exact recounting of the facts of my life, I have tried to recapture something of the spirit of my involvement with animation. The odd and wonderful and curious truth is this: the animated cartoons I directed are now the facts—my report cards. The varied memories of their origins are often, and perhaps rightfully so, fictional.

For me the startling, unbelievable matter is this: when I was nineteen years old, somebody offered to pay me to draw. For over fifty years and over 250 films, other somebodies have, amazingly, persisted in continuing to reward me for doing what I love to do.

NOTE: For those who seek a chronological thread, no matter how thin, on which to hang the following facts and figuratives, I nervously recommend the Appendix.

Homes deducting the bally old income tax

Johnson and the Birth of a Notion

"**W**hy do animated cartoonists use animals?" For the same reason that Aesop, La Fontaine, Kipling, Beatrix Potter, and Kenneth Grahame did: it is easier and more believable to humanize animals than it is to humanize humans.

A young man came to work with us at Warner Bros. Cartoons as a writer shortly after World War II and promptly and proudly wrote home to his grandmother in Denver that he was writing scripts for Bugs Bunny.

"I can't understand why you're writing scripts for Bugs Bunny," the old lady replied with some asperity. "He's funny enough just as he is."

Believability. That is what we were striving for. Not believability by the audience; that will follow. But belief in the life of characters—by the writer, the artist, the director, the animator. That, after all, is the dictionary definition and meaning of the word "animation": to invoke life.

What was implicit in what the old lady was saying was that our job was not to *invent* what Bugs Bunny did but to *report* his doings. Just as I, at seven, upon reading *Tom Sawyer*, would have been outraged at the suggestion that Mark Twain or anybody else *invented* Tom and Huckleberry Finn and their company. Tom Sawyer *happened*. He was not imaginary. He was *real*. He still is real. What else can he be but real? And there can be no doubt that Mark Twain shared that belief.

Johnson at ease

Character *always* comes first, before the physical representation. Just as it is with all living things, including human beings. We are not what we look like. We are not even what we sound like. We are how we move; in other words, our personalities. And our personalities are shaped by what we think, by where we come from, by what we have experienced. And that personality is unique to each of us.

Up to the advent of Johnson, I had little reason to doubt that the differences between cats were purely visual: size, color, sex (although sexual differences in cats seemed to be a secret guarded well by cats; I was not a precocious child at seven—just curious). If there were personality differences, I was unaware of them until Johnson padded in on little fog feet and taught me that first and most important lesson of animation: individuality. Yes, in looking back, I can see that it all began with Johnson, because Johnson demonstrated with such vivid certainty the whole truth of the matter: *it is the individual, the oddity, the peculiarity that counts.* If Johnson had stood up, which was unlikely since he was a cat, and pounded on the rostrum with his shoe, he could not have made his point more clearly to my seven-year-old mind: the only things worth watching in this or any other world are those that identify and overcome the ordinary. That summer morning in Balboa was a turning point for a small boy whose thoughts up to that time were concerned, like his cousin the shark, only with gastronomic matters.

And so I was all unaware that the first step in my destiny to become an animation director would come silently out of a salmon-pink dawn, each step leaving a small, precise, dry paw print on the dew-moist sand. Through the gray salt-rimed boards of our back fence he moved with the self-assured, liquid, dignified delicacy of a world-class welterweight.

With my fascinated nose waffled against the rust-brown

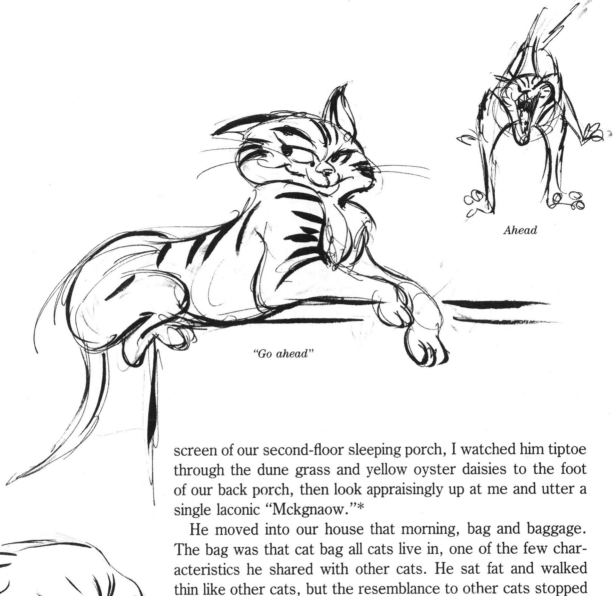

"Go ahead"

Ahead

*Johnson
and worldly
possessions*

screen of our second-floor sleeping porch, I watched him tiptoe through the dune grass and yellow oyster daisies to the foot of our back porch, then look appraisingly up at me and utter a single laconic "Mckgnaow."*

He moved into our house that morning, bag and baggage. The bag was that cat bag all cats live in, one of the few characteristics he shared with other cats. He sat fat and walked thin like other cats, but the resemblance to other cats stopped there.

His baggage was what appeared to be a very old, very used tongue depressor, fastened securely about his neck with a bit of tarry string, bearing in violet indelible ink the crude inscription: JOHNSON. Whether this was his name, that of his former proprietors, or his blood type we were unable to determine, since he discussed his past not at all and responded to the name Johnson as well as any other, which was not at all; actually

* *From James Joyce's* Ulysses, *but Johnson said it first.*

15

going in response to that name
only to my mother and then only
when she offered him grapefruit.

"MCKGNAOW"
3

For it cannot be denied that
Johnson was a patsy for grapefruit.
Many a battered mouse owed his
life and his continued livelihood
to an unknown grapefruit
offered to Johnson by my
mother. Johnson would
leave a Bismarck herring,
a stick of catnip, or a
decayed sea gull for a single
wedge of grapefruit. For a whole grapefruit, he would have
committed fraud or practiced usury.

I can only suppose that some vital juice necessary to cats
was in short supply in the muttering Ferrari-like bowels of
Johnson. He could easily devour a grapefruit a quarter his size
at a sitting. Mother discovered this curious facet of Johnson's
metabolism one day at breakfast when Johnson sauntered up
to the table and suggested sharing her breakfast, with his most
ingratiating "Mckgnaow." Mother, who was easily flattered,

*Johnson
and the Great
Grapefruit Wars*

16

AND RECEIVING IT

offered him a bit of bacon, a scrap of buttered toast, and the edge of egg white that remained on her plate, but Johnson insisted that she misunderstood his needs. After a brief conversation in different languages, my mother reluctantly offered Johnson the remains of her grapefruit.

There are historic moments, similar in nature to the Curies' quantum leap from the sight of glowing pitchblende to the discovery of radium. That morning our family witnessed just such a moment. There was a sudden electric blue crack in the atmosphere like those preceding a tornado, as Johnson went at that innocent grapefruit like a tangerine-colored buzz saw: as the stripped shell of the fruit spun slowly to a stop like a twisting coin, Johnson sat staring dreamy-eyed, dreamy-grinned at Mother. As the reamed-out grapefruit rind whirled to a long loping stop, Johnson's lox-pink tongue tenderly flicked a final golden drop from a whisker and whispered to Mother the single English word he knew: "More."

Johnson's normal "Mckgnaow" had the same lisping slur later made popular by Humphrey Bogart, and like Bogart, his vocal impediment was due to a deadened nerve in his split upper lip. This honorable scar left a small Gothic window through which peered a scythe-like fang to inform the world that Johnson was not a cat to be trifled with. Mark Twain said that if you carried a cat home by the tail you would get information that would be valuable to you all your life. Such information could more conveniently be obtained by meddling with Johnson's tongue depressor.

Whatever else it represented, that bit of tongue depressor was Johnson's sole possession: his entire estate, his chattel, his treasure. It was all he had to leave to his eldest son, and he treated it as a sacred object. Any attempt to remove it resulted in what can only be described as a physical threat of the most nerve-racking implications. Touch his treasure and Johnson simply went into a lightning somersault, coupled with a full-bodied, four-footed karate chop, in which the meddler suddenly found his hand caught in an inverted cat vise of sixteen needle-pointed claws, the offending hand flat against Johnson's stomach, his eyes cobra-like, scythe-like slits of pure malevolence—one of Johnson's feline canines caught on his lower lip, its amethyst point devoid of dentine, sharp as a scalpel, blue as a diamond. At this point the disturber of sacred tongue depressors was unharmed, but the slightest move elicited a corresponding slight extension of those sixteen curved stilettos. It was not unlike having one's hand in a boxing glove full of fishhooks. If one wanted to get out—and one did—it would require the minimal help of four fearless human assistants of

In dubious combat

18

*Johnson's invention of
the space helmet*

fantastic manual dexterity. It was possible to escape only if these assistants moved with split-second, simultaneous accuracy to pull Johnson's paws apart. This method allowed one to escape with only minor wounds, but the safest yet and most unnerving way was to wait it out until Johnson had made up his mind that you were only kidding. This might take from five minutes to a half hour and few people had that kind of courage or were that free of panic or hysteria. So most unfortunates tried to snatch the hand free immediately upon being trapped, with results too bloodily ineffectual to be described. Only a half grapefruit gently dropped over his face like an ether cone would relax Johnson enough so his claws, like spines of a cactus, could be individually picked from the threatened extremity.

While half a grapefruit would anesthetize Johnson, the most interesting way of serving Johnson his passion fruit was to present it to him in its glorious entirety: a whole unsullied, uncut, large grapefruit. The curved surface was too difficult for Johnson to achieve an effective toothhold, or clawhold; its broad surface was as difficult as it would be for a human being to try

*A cat swimming
is not a pleasant object*

*A source of sheer
terror to small dogs
and old ladies*

to bite a watermelon. It took him many frustrating hours of chasing grapefruits fruitlessly around the house before he recognized the wisdom of trapping it by dribbling this elusive adversary to the nearest corner. There it became possible for him to scratch a small flap of rind and thus burrow greedily in, ripping the innards out of the hapless fruit, often ending up with three-quarters of the rind cocked over his face like a small space helmet.

On such occasions he seemed to enjoy this raffish adornment and would saunter out onto the sand, often with only one eye visible under the overhang, a curious sight to many people, a delight to our family, and a source of sheer terror to small dogs and old ladies.

And so Johnson's first lesson to me as a future animator was this: Eschew the ordinary, disdain the commonplace. If you have a single-minded need for something, let it be the unusual, the esoteric, the bizarre, the unexpected, such as a cat hooked on grapefruit. Somewhere along the line I realized that my insatiable and seldom-satisfied appetite for tuna fish, deviled eggs, popcorn, Delaware Punch, and sex never got me any points on the notoriety scale; too many people shared these appetites. Johnson demonstrated by precept, not pedantry, that only the peculiar will get you anywhere: if there are ten pictures hanging on the wall, only the one off-balance will get much attention, if only because it makes people uneasy, which can also be useful.

20

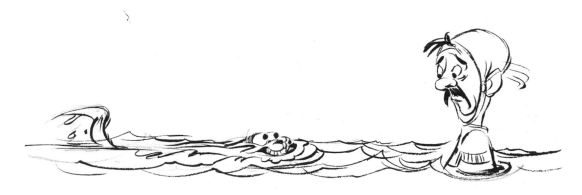

If it had only been grapefruit, I might have missed the lesson, but I could never have overlooked another interesting facet of Johnson's many-faceted character.

He liked to swim in the ocean.

I mean, all the evidence so indicated. It may have been because he was gregarious. It may have been that he didn't want to miss out on anything that looked interesting. That last possibility, too, has stayed with me all my life and I choose to believe that was Johnson's reason for plunging into the surf whenever we did so.

Now, a cat swimming is not a pleasant object. No matter how high his degree of enjoyment, he still looks as if he is strangling. Eyes pop with a wild hysterical bulge; teeth grit under lips that gape back to his armpits; ears flatten back until he seems more like a hairy strangulated moray eel caught in a wringer than he does anything remotely feline. Cats also swim low in the water with just their gaping jaws and popping, evil, frightening eyes visible, leaving a slippery oily wake of gull feathers and grapefruit seeds.

Actually, Johnson must have thought his expression to be benign and friendly, and, to be sure, he purred reassuringly as he approached a swimmer. His purr, however, was underwater and the resultant sloshing and gurgling only enhanced the picture of a strangling creature spewed up from the Great Barrier Reef.

*Old Cat of the Sea
and uncertain associate*

In those days, swimming suits for both sexes had partly covered shoulders, somewhat like a middy blouse, so when Johnson tired, his roost while at sea was the nearest shoulder—family, if available; stranger if need be. Strangers, he found, must be approached from the rear, since a frontal approach

Johnson with sister Dorothy and brother Charles, who obstructs a clear view of Johnson's notorious brick cat house, Balboa, California, 1918

always resulted in hysteria. Johnson disliked emotional turmoil of any kind, yet he never quite learned that climbing on a stranger's shoulder, even from the rear, was bound to have eruptive consequences.

When people came staggering spastically out of the surf at Balboa beach, every nerve string jangling a chorus of gibbering fright, mouths sputtering in monosyllabic incoherence, we knew that Johnson had approached them.

Occasionally Johnson, with his grapefruit helmet stuck firmly on his head, would wander drunkenly down the beach picking up tar, bits of dead sea gulls, and, on one notable occasion, bumping blindly into a picnic of YWCA girls. These young ladies did not recognize Johnson as a cat in his space helmet. They fled panic-stricken into the surf and Johnson went in after them. The YWCA did not come back to Balboa again.

22

One day I had the misfortune to fall off the back porch and into the brick shelter we had built for Johnson. Three things resulted from this entirely innocent accident. My mother, horrified when she saw me holding my oddly limp right arm, called the doctor, who came over and set a broken bone. "Greenstick fracture," the doctor said to my proud ears.

When my father came home that night, he asked my mother what had "happened to Charles." When he found out, he took me on a long round of his favorite saloons, filling himself with whiskey, me with sarsaparilla, and boasting to everyone in sight that, at the tender age of seven, his son had broken his arm falling in a cat house.

The third thing that happened was that the following morning we discovered paw prints in the sand leading away from this semi-demolished cat house out over the wet sand to the sea. Perhaps that was where Johnson came from in the first place.

Johnson was indeed a cat for all seasons and all fortunes and I was generously allowed to share one summer season with him. I like to think that if I had not fallen on his house, breaking my arm and his contemplation, he might be with me yet. Perhaps not. But I am sure that on some grapefruit ranch by some distant sea, Johnson lives on. Although he wore a cat uniform, he contemptuously disdained all forms of feline behavior—an immortal, surely; an individual absolutely.

Uncle Lynn's Stubborn Liver: Comic Tales and Comic Stars

Strange when you come to think of it, that of all the countless folk who have lived before our time on this planet not one is known in history or in legend as having died of laughter.

— MAX BEERBOHM

Merriment in Sherwood Forest: ROBIN HOOD DAFFY (1958)

A dear uncle told me once, when I was deep in despair at some injustice by some bureaucrat, scholastic or familial, "Chuck, they can kill you, but they're not allowed to eat you." Exactly why this statement has since stood as the cornerpost of my determination to live my life as a life and not as an apology, only Ralph Waldo Emerson could have explained. And I hadn't read much Emerson when I was eleven.

Uncle Lynn. The perfect uncle. The ne-plus-ultra uncle. Even his name was, and is, perfect. It never was Uncle Lynn, of course; it was Unclynn. Dogs and boys loved and trusted him. He thought like a boy, or a dog, and he was of adult size, which we were not, and could implement such thought with action. His fancies were those of a dog, or a boy, and he never ques-

Waiting for Godot—
Claude Cat, that is

tioned those impulses. If a mule-drawn dump cart passed, full high with moist red earth, he immediately engaged in comparing notes with the driver. He was *always* able to compare notes with anyone, human or animal. He always had something in common with every dog, cat, turtle, sea gull, child, or man. He had somehow, somewhere, someway done something they, too, had done, and from this common ground an uncommon miracle always occurred: two average small boys and one average small dog digging luxuriating toes into that same lofty loamy lovely dirt, as Uncle Lynn talked to the enchanted driver about Missouri mules, Malayan buffalo, hickory shafts, goatskin hames, and rattail files. As for the two small boys and the one small dog, they guarded the surprise and pretended that they did not know of the false bottom in the old wooden dray that would send us tumbling into the landfill when the driver pulled the long wooden release bar. And after we had scrambled clear, he would look back down with surprise. "Lost 'em," Uncle Lynn would say. "Guess we'll have to go back and get some more boys." "And a dog," the driver would add. "Load's not complete without a dog." That's the effect Uncle Lynn had on some people (and on *all* dogs and boys, of course). They became part of the enactment of fancies that only dogs and boys and Uncle Lynn understood.

Greeting Godot

"Scaring the Tennis Ball"—
a highly technical game:
TWO'S A CROWD (1950)

26

Six points!

I remember all of us listening with the most slavish love to Uncle Lynn's stories. He never disappointed us, the ending was all a small boy could hope for: there was never a hint of morality, no overt heavy-handed effort to make us better children, better adults, or better at anything except learning the love of listening.

"This friend of mine," said Uncle Lynn, "was a swordfish strangler out of San Diego Harbor. After the marlins and broadtails were brought aboard the fishing smack *The Drunken Nymph*, his job was to strangle the swordfish. Dirty job, but somebody had to do it. Name of Wiltford. Only swordfish strangler I ever knew by that name," said Uncle Lynn. We nodded our approval of the logic, we had never known a swordfish strangler named Wiltford either. "Actually," continued Uncle Lynn, "his name was Wiltferd W. Wiltford, last name had an

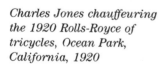

Charles Jones chauffeuring the 1920 Rolls-Royce of tricycles, Ocean Park, California, 1920

Criminally minded fake newsboy, Balboa beach, circa 1918

The Shropshire Slasher:
DEDUCE, YOU SAY (1956)

28

Angelo, the world's strongest flea: TO ITCH HIS OWN *(1958)*

'o' in the 'ford' part, first name an 'e' in the 'ford' part. Well, I don't know whether it was working around fish or not, but he developed a severe case of liver trouble. Worst case of liver trouble he'd ever seen, said Wiltferd's doctor, looking solemn, the way doctors always look whenever they diagnose liver trouble or a strangulated pimple or an ingrown earlobe. Couldn't offer a cure or even an easement—too advanced, he said. Sorry and all that.

"I don't know how many of you have carried around a troubled liver." Uncle Lynn looked carefully around at us, seemed reassured by what he saw, and continued. "Well, Wiltferd had to cut down on swordfish strangling except on weekends and na-

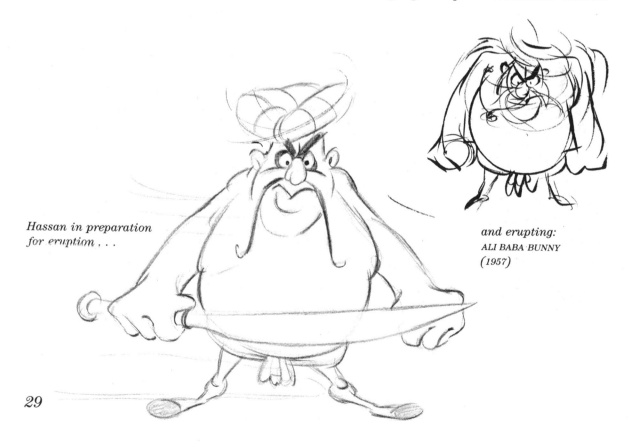

Hassan in preparation for eruption . . .

and erupting: ALI BABA BUNNY *(1957)*

29

tional holidays. He was a Sixth-Day Adventist, hadn't quite made it to the seventh, so he didn't have to observe religious holidays. So what he'd do, as a matter of courtesy, was to strangle half a swordfish or half strangle a whole swordfish. Takes practice, that," said Uncle Lynn, nodding his approval at us. "But nevertheless old Wiltferd got weaker and weaker liver-wise and he got despondent, too, because by contrast everybody else in his body—spleen, lights, heart, all the valves, esophagus—were all going top speed and on all eight cylinders. He thought it would be a pity, did old Wiltferd, who was knocking eighty at the time (oldest swordfish strangler south of San Luis Obispo), it would be a pity and a shame if a two-bit liver would put all those other organs out of business. So as a kind of therapy he went up into the mountains behind San Diego and strangled a bear and two Gila monsters. But it didn't seem to help and he'd just about given up when he met this Indian, name of Forgot-to-go-to-Meeting Smith, who was considered by many locals as an authority on livers and liver ailments. Wiltferd endeared himself to Forgot-to-go-to-Meeting Smith by strangling a tarantula that had taken up residence in Forgot-to-go-to-Meeting Smith's pants, and had become a source of some irritation to Forgot-to-go-to-Meeting Smith, he was grateful indeed to Wiltferd.

"So, to show his gratitude to Wiltferd, Forgot-to-go-to-Meeting Smith concocted this liver-leavening medicine made of wolfbane, owlbane, Indian paintbrush, cowbane, shredded wheat, poison oak, wildcat bane, and the blood of unborn acorns.

"Well, you know," Uncle Lynn said (obviously relieved that relief was at hand for Wiltferd Wiltford), "Wiltferd drank three gallons of that medicine, which by the way you can't get over the counter, and immediately his liver hauled up its braces, snapped to attention, and started everybody up at 5 a.m. on double time. Talk about pushy livers, this liver ran Wiltferd's

Ralph Phillips studying:
FROM A TO Z-Z-Z-Z (1954)

30

Nasty Canasta in a fleeting moment of victory at cards:
BARBARY COAST BUNNY (1956)

insides like Black Jack Pershing's first platoon. No nonsense, shape up or ship out. Oh, that liver was a taskmaster, but in all fairness, it never asked anything of any other organ that it wouldn't do itself. However, whatever—time took its toll, and in spite of all this admirable liver's power, strength, and will, every other organ gradually deteriorated, and one day, like the wonderful one-horse shay, the whole lot of them gave up, handed in their uniforms, and Wiltferd Wiltford died before his time at one hundred and seven. Every organ died with him, every one, that is, but that magnificent liver. After Wiltferd died, they had to take it out and kill it with a club."

We were all at peace with the world and ready for bed after such a wonderful, *believable* story with such a satisfactory ending, each of us sleepily wishing that we could have been there to help chase down that wonderful liver.

My Father and
the English Language

"A fellow uncurbed, unfettered, uncontrolled of speech, un-periphrastic, bombastic, loquacious."

> — **MY FATHER**, QUOTING ARISTOPHANES
> (448–385 B.C.) IN SUPPORT OF HIS
> DETESTATION OF WARREN GAMALIEL HARDING

The dethpicable Warren Gamaliel Harding

When I was still young enough to believe that you were not allowed by federal law to dislike, much less detest, the President of the United States, my father detested Warren Gamaliel Harding.

This worried me. Having my father clapped into a federal prison for treachery or treason might just call attention to me and the crime of being his son and might send me to reform school, the Siberia of boyhood.

Father's reason for considering Warren Gamaliel Harding despicable (the word would show up years later in Daffy Duck's mouth as "dethpicable") was not because he was a crook—that was to be expected—but because of his grotesque sloppiness in his slander of the English language. If Robert Frost's lumbermen could only judge a man by the way he handled an ax, Father would only judge the intellect of a man (or a woman) by the way he or she handled words.

"Warren Gamaliel Harding," he grunted angrily, "shovels words with the same lack of respect we would show in shoveling manure. As long as it sounds portentous, it doesn't matter to him if it has meaning. He doesn't know the meaning of the word 'meaning.' "

Recently I came across an example of the kind of ostentation that so enraged my father. This from Harding's first Inaugural speech:* "When one surveys the world about him after the great storm, noting the marks of destruction and yet rejoicing in the raggedness of the things that withstood it, if he is an American, he breathes the clarified atmosphere with a strange mixture of regret and new hope . . . standing in this presence, mindful of the solemnity of the occasion, feeling the emotions which no one more is a public mandate in manifest understanding." No wonder H. L. Mencken described Harding's prose style as a "hippopotamus struggling to free itself from a slough of molasses."

H. L. Mencken's description of W. G. Harding's prose

"Mush! Mush!" My father was on the verge of imploding. "If a man cannot manage his native language, how can he manage his native land? *Who* is he talking about? *What* is he talking about, and *when* is he talking about it?

"Listen." He snatched up a book, although he probably didn't need it. " 'Once, on a glittering ice-field, ages and ages ago, Ung, a maker of pictures, fashioned an image of snow.' That's Rudyard Kipling! Everything you need to know about his subject, Cro-Magnon man: Who. What. When. Where. In poetic form! In one sentence! And later in the same poem, describing the rest of the tribe: 'Men of the berg-battered beaches, men of the boulder-hatched hill' . . . Doesn't that sing? Doesn't that evoke a wonderful, powerful image of what it was *like* in the ice age?"

"Ung, a maker of pictures"

Indeed it did, and indeed it does today, those words pound like surf, and thrust aside all the mealymouthed slop of the Warren Gamaliel Hardings of the world.

One fateful day our family moved into a rented house, furnished with a complete set of Mark Twain, and my life changed

---

* Although it is not a parody but a real speech, I found it, curiously enough, in a book called Parodies.

Mark my words, this is my dearest friend

forever. What grapefruit was to Johnson the cat, Mark Twain became to me.

For instance:

Mark Twain used words the way the graphic artist uses line control. He was terribly afraid of what he called his "darlings." That is: phrases of such delicious mushy grandeur and mellifluous cadence that they protruded from the clean line of his prose like a puce Christmas tree. He "murdered his darlings" without mercy, but admitting to the same agony that we all feel when we sense that what we see in our drawing is more than is there. Dorothy Parker said it more clearly after seeing a brilliantly pageanted, dull musical comedy called *Jumbo*. "There is less here than meets the eye," she said. Tattoo that across your reluctant retina and you will never confuse superficial technique with the subject matter at hand.

I first became interested in the Coyote while devouring Mark Twain's *Roughing It* at the age of seven. I had heard of the coyote only in passing references from passing adults and thought of it—if I thought of it at all—as a sort of dissolute collie. As it turned out, that's just about what a coyote is, and no one saw it more clearly than Mark Twain.

"The coyote is a long, slim, sick and sorry-looking skeleton, with a gray wolf-skin stretched over it, a tolerably bushy tail

*The Coyote—
Mark Twain discovered
him first*

LIGHT TEXTURED

34

that forever sags down with a despairing expression of forsakenness and misery, a furtive and evil eye, and a long, sharp face, with slightly lifted lip and exposed teeth. He has a general slinking expression all over. The coyote is a living, breathing allegory of Want. He is *always* hungry. He is always poor, out of luck and friendless . . . even the fleas would desert him for a velocipede . . . He does not mind going a hundred miles to breakfast, and a hundred and fifty to dinner, because he is sure to have three or four days between meals, and he can just as well be traveling and looking at the scenery as lying around doing nothing and adding to the burdens of his parents."

Boy meets protagonist

Who could resist such an enchanting creature? He and I had so much in common! Rushing to the encyclopedia, I found our measurements to be about the same, too: four feet long in our stocking feet; weight about fifty pounds stripped (fur long and coarse, grizzled buff below and sun-bleached whitish above—a minor detail). But the clincher was this: "Noted for its nightly serenades of short yaps and mournful yowls." That was me all right, I had been assured too often by parents and siblings alike that my nocturnal serenades consisted of short yaps and mournful yowls.

I cannot begin to express the relief I felt at finding a companion to my own unique ineptness. It was so reassuring to find someone else of my own age (another characteristic we

Heavy tipper and bullion:
ALI BABA BUNNY (1957)

shared was our age: between seven and eight) who also could be a burden to his parents. I was beginning to believe that I was a failure in life, and to find a colorfully inept companion was a happy and stunning surprise.

I wish I had known then what I found to be true many years later: that comedy is nearly always the stuff of the ordinary, concerning itself with simple matters and simple ambitions, with ordinary pursuits and ordinary ambitions.

Charlie Chaplin often, and the Coyote always, is simply trying to get something to eat. Daffy Duck, Jack Benny, and indeed Woody Allen are simply trying for human dignity, recognition, and, with Benny and Daffy, the added need to save or get a little money in the process. Daffy and Jack will try to explain this need to the audience. Daffy, after betraying Bugs Bunny to a huge forty-foot-high Abominable Snowman, says, "Sure, I know it's a rotten thing to do, but better it should happen to him than to me. I'm different from other people—pain hurts me." Or Jack Benny accused of penury by Mary Livingston. "When you had appendicitis," she said, "you asked Rochester if he would do the operation."

"I did *not*," Benny replied angrily. "I only asked him if he *could* do the operation."

Think of how simple and recognizable the needs are of all comedians: food, housing, love, the protection of another unfortunate, the eternal battle to find rationality within the establishment . . . always from the lowliest rung on the ladder.

In all Bugs Bunny films we opened on Bugs in a simple, understandable, and rational place for a rabbit to be: in the forest, in the meadow, down a hole, in a carrot patch, or in a pet store . . . but above all else living peaceably, contemplating an obscure Wang Dynasty dissertation on carrots—a sort of Professor Higgins in sweet solitude.

Then along comes someone with designs on his hide, his foot, his use as a meal or as an outer-space rocket passenger. It is a very simple formula. Bugs resists in every way he can imagine, and he is a very imaginative rabbit. He is also that

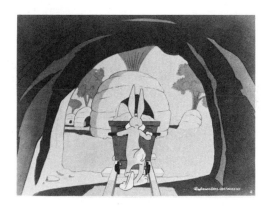

Establishing a carrot mine

Singing "Bunny-Crack Corn" in land of Paul Bunyan: LUMBER JACK-RABBIT *(1954)*

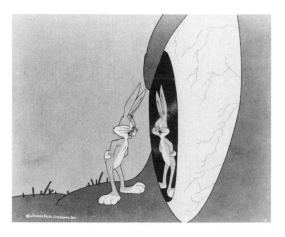

Discussing the matter with Bunyan's dog, K-9000

37

Everyman Fudd

unusual comedian: a comic hero, and they are very few. Bugs *is* what I would like to be: debonair, quick-witted, very fast on the comeback, a sort of male Dorothy Parkerish D'Artagnan.

Most of our other characters are not noted for triumph. Inept contenders with the problems of life: Wile E. Coyote, Elmer Fudd, Yosemite Sam, Daffy Duck, Foghorn Leghorn, Sylvester Cat, like Chaplin, Keaton, Woody Allen, Donald Duck, Goofy, Tom (of Tom 'n' Jerry), Richard Pryor, are all mistake-prone, low men on a short and poorly carved totem pole. We recognize their simple ambitions. Their public mistakes, I think, help compensate for or at least make understandable our own private mistakes.

Genius frustratus hoist on his own intellect

"I never met a man worse than I am."

— GEORGE ORWELL

I never had to leave home to develop any character I ever developed or helped to develop. All I had to do was reach down inside my own self and there lurking was the essence of Daffy Duck, the Coyote, or Elmer, or the Martian. It was simply a matter of bringing it to the surface.

We are all Daffy Ducks, Woody Allens, Chaplins, and Coyotes inside. We are all haplessly and hopelessly hopeful. We are all to some extent avaricious, mean, traitorous, envious, jealous—but most of these charming characteristics we manage to keep fairly well buried and under control. If, however, one breaks out, we become tragedians. If we keep it under control, we remain comedians. If we are not all of us incipient comedians, why do we laugh at comedy? Why do we love great comedians? Not for what they look like, but for what they *do* . . . They are mirrors of what we do, or, in the case of the comic hero, what we would like to be able to do.

Among our stable we had very few comic heroes: Bugs Bunny, Pepé Le Pew, Tweety Bird, and the Road Runner about does it. The hero is what we would like to be, and so we cheer him on, hoping to emulate him but ruefully acknowledging that we probably will not. But the comic hero does extend the hope, the outside possibility that we, too, can swagger through life with the dashing assurance of an Errol Flynn, the wit of a Mencken, and the beguiling innocence of a Groucho Marx.

Pepé Le Pew and love potion: CAT'S BAH *(1954)*

How To Become An Animator

Embryonic animator and vital tools of his trade

We always had books in the house we lived in. We not only had books, we had books (old or new) that were fresh to us. The way it worked was this: a house in those days of the early twenties had books. Incredible as it seems, that's what people did: they read. They read books and they talked to each other about what they'd read. We didn't have a phonograph until I was twelve, a radio until I was seventeen, or television until I was forty-six.

So that left books. When you rented a furnished house, it was equipped with furniture and books. So when we were ready to move, Father would scout around for a furnished house.

41

Sniffles and the Bookworm in 1940

"Furnished" in his lexicon meant furnished with books, hundreds being mandatory, thousands being preferable. Colonel Terhune's big house on the Speedway in Ocean Park had thousands of books, as did *Times* editor Harry Carr's place on Mount Washington Drive, so the six or seven or eight of our family stayed in each house for over five years, until we had exhausted the supply, a sort of omnivorous plague of indiscriminate readers. If it was worthwhile for someone to print, it was worthwhile for us to read. Trash and treasure are soon separable to the inveterate reader, and we all learned this vital difference by experience, not by the force of an adult's opinion. I read through Horatio Alger with derision and hoots of mocking laughter, I read through Stephen Leacock with joy and joyous laughter.

"It's simple," my father had quoted. "The truth is tart, the

Our wild-eyed brooding place: 115 Wadsworth Avenue, 1919–23

false is sweet." Well, maybe, I thought, then what about candy? It took struggle, but I began to realize the difference between something sticky and sweet on your tongue and something sweet and sticky on your brain. Ergo (I had just discovered the word), I could enjoy something sweet on my taste buds without thinking much about it, but it was entirely impossible for me to read a book without thinking, and reading *The Bobbsey Twins*, for instance, made me think of throwing up.

Mother not only loved books, she truly loved children and she loved bearing children. The term "natural childbirth" would have had little meaning; to her, there was no other kind. What bleating lambs are to Bengal tigers, Old Grand-Dad to many old granddads, the opposite sex to a fortunate few, having babies was to Mother. As I remember it, there was always the ebb and flow of countless children milling around our houses, wearing each other's stockings, pants, and prejudices. I was

The charming hostel in
CLAWS FOR ALARM (1954)

43

Charles Adams Jones, exhibiting a sense of false security and ease in Spokane, Washington, before the birth of his first son

Mabel McQuiddy Martin Jones, in a moment of uncertainty about the validity of motherhood

seldom privy to which of these moppets were siblings and which were infant Mahomets who had gravitated quite naturally to the soft mountain of love that was Mother. But out of this teeming infantile anthill, at least four of us grew up to be graphic artists of one kind or another:

Margaret Barbara Jones, master weaver and designer, teacher and fabric designer; Dorothy Jane Jones, sculptor, writer, and illustrator; Richard Kent Jones, painter, photographer, teacher, and printmaker; and Charles Martin Jones, animator and animated-cartoon director. Why? Why us? Observation sadly compels us to realize that love alone is not enough—would that it were. No, there is always some oddity in the infant environment of the artist, some peculiarity unique to that environment.

Youngest child ever to be run out of Spokane, Washington, on a rail

In our case it was Father.

Father loved his children but hated having a family. He became belatedly aware one dismal rain-struck morning of the painful reality of his fatherhood: that he was up to his hips in children, and unless he wanted to blame those selfsame hips which were, after all, responsible, he must do something to rectify matters. In short, get out.

Now, all that remained for him was the technicality of how to do so. We were far from a wealthy family. Indeed, a history of Father's fiscal meanderings would make a valuable contribution to the "What to Avoid" chapter of any "How to Succeed" textbook. In short, he didn't have enough bread to supply bread for his family for the next twelve to fifteen years, much less provide all the gear, from garter belts to saddle shoes, necessary to see the self-respecting child through high school and, perhaps, college.

*Portrait of the cartoonist as
a fake baby, 1913*

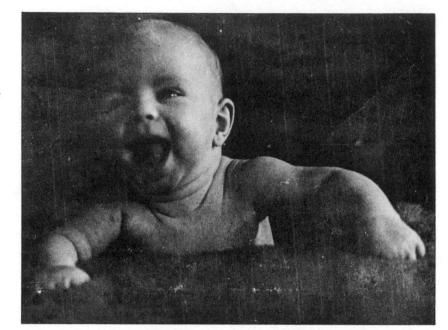

*Mabel M. Jones and
Charles M. Jones, 1913*

*Dorothy Jane Jones: in the
history of man, the only
older sister to be genuinely
fond of a younger brother,
Ocean Park, 1920*

Ocean Park, 1920

Margaret Barbara Jones   Katherine Cone (cousin)   Richard Kent Jones

Dorothy Jane Jones   Charles Martin Jones   John Cone (cousin)

*Annandale
Grammar School
harboring a misfit
(at left, second row),
1923*

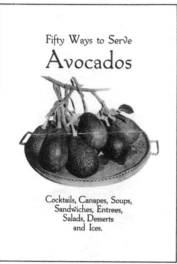

Fifty Ways to Serve

Avocados

Cocktails, Canapes, Soups,
Sandwiches, Entrees,
Salads, Desserts
and Ices.

*My father's book
on avocados*

The only solution seemed to be to strike it rich. Then he could run for the hills, secure in the knowledge that his family was fiscally secure.

"Striking It Rich" in Southern California in the 1920s was not at all unusual. Indeed, along with the bizarre crop of intriguing new religious cults that thrived so well in our desert soil, it was a way of life. Opportunities for immediate wealth were a dime a dozen—and worth approximately that. Father tried them all, plus some introductory ideas of his own: he formed companies that attempted to sell avocados when people called them Alligator Pears and thought of them as either poisonous or Com-

---

AVOCADOS FOR HEALTH

Plain Avocado Omelette

Allow ½ c. finely diced avocado to two eggs. Prepare eggs and seasoning in manner usual for omelette. When ready to turn, scatter avocado over omelette, fold and place in oven for short time.

DESSERTS

Avocado Tutti Frutti

Chop and mix apples, oranges, peaches, pineapple, bananas and dates. Add an equal amount of diced avocado. Make a syrup of the fruit juices, adding small amount of water if necessary, and pour over fruit. Serve in sherbet glasses with whipped cream and ground nut meats. Chill before serving.

Avocado Sundae

Mash a ripe avocado and whip to a creamy consistency, adding 1 tsp. powdered sugar and 1 tsp. ground nut meats for each tbsp. avocado cream. Pour over any ice cream just before serving.

Avocado and Date Whip

Cream the meat of an avocado, add a few drops lemon juice and mix with finely ground dates, beating together thoroughly. Chill and serve in sherbet glasses. Top with red or green maraschino cherry and pour a tsp. of maraschino liquor over each portion.

Avocado and Banana Whip

Press 6 ripe bananas and equal amount of avocado meat through a puree sieve. Add 4 tbsp. lemon juice, 4 tbsp. sugar and 1 c. walnut meats, chopped finely. Chill thoroughly and serve in sherbet glasses covered with whipped cream.

The Aristocrat of Fruits

AVOCADOS FOR WEALTH

Avocado Souffle

Put an avocado through sieve. Beat whites of three eggs, add ½ c. sugar, few drops lemon juice, and avocado pulp. Mix, put in lightly buttered baking dish and bake in moderate oven for 15 minutes, or until firm, setting dish in shallow pan of boiling water. Custard cups can be used in place of baking dish.

Avocado Meringue Pie

Mix 6 oz. sugar, 4 eggs, 2 c. rich milk and maple flavoring. Add 6 oz. avocado meat pulped or finely diced. Pour into pie crust and bake. Cover with meringue and brown.

Avocado Cake

Add ½ c. chopped dates to 1 c. mashed avocado and 1 c. whipped cream, sweetened and flavored with vanilla. Spread this as filling between very thin layers of plain layer cake, garnishing top with nuts or chopped candied cherries.

Avocado Ice Cream No. 1

To creamed pulp of 8 medium-size avocados add 1 lb. sugar, ½ gallon cream, 1 tsp. almond flavoring. Mix thoroughly and freeze.

Avocado Ice Cream No. 2

Make a boiled custard of the yolks of 5 eggs, 1 qt. milk, 2 c. sugar, flavoring with vanilla or pistachio extract. When cool add creamed pulp of 6 small avocados and freeze.

The Aristocrat of Fruits

munistic or both; he offered vineyards for sale when Prohibition was in full astringent swing; he took a short option on a place called Signal Hill and tried frustratingly to grow geraniums there for the Eastern market, only to discover years later that his floral nonfecundity was caused by crude oil saturating the soil. Where flowers should have blossomed, crude-oil rigs sprouted instead, long after Father's geraniums and options had withered away.

But—now listen—every time Father started a new business, he did three things: 1. He bought a new suit. 2. He bought acres of the finest Hammermill bond stationery, complete with the company's letterhead. 3. He bought hundreds of boxes of pencils, also complete with the company name. (There were ashtrays so embellished, too, but this had nothing to do with my becoming an animator.) Ah, but what *did* have to do with my becoming an animator and my siblings becoming graphic artists is this:

EVERY TIME FATHER'S
BUSINESS FAILED, HIS CHILDREN INHERITED
A FRESH LEGACY OF THE FINEST DRAWING
MATERIALS IMAGINABLE.

Where every other child on the block was lucky once a month to get a measly little shoddy little tablet made of measly and shoddy newsprint, probably adorned with a picture on the front cover of a dyspeptic lion or a hideous mewling child, and, if very lucky, was reluctantly doled a horrible little penny pencil about as useful for drawing as a dental pick, we Joneses were rolling in tons of lovely white bond paper and the finest Ticonderoga pencils.

NOT ONLY THAT!

We were forbidden—actually forbidden—to draw on both sides of the paper. Because, of course, Father wanted to get rid of the stationery from a defunct business as soon as possible, and he brought logic to bear in sustaining his viewpoint: "You never know when you're going to make a good drawing," he said. And then, stretching credulity to the point of idiocy: "Suppose you were Leonardo da Vinci and you painted the *Mona Lisa* on one side of your canvas and *The Last Supper* on the other—how would you ever hang it?" Nevertheless—and perhaps, just perhaps, he knew what he was saying—he brought into focus a most vital rule of creativity: You must, if you ever would pretend to artistry, respect your medium; be it a blank piece of paper or canvas, an untouched bar sheet, an uncarved piece of stone, or an unexposed frame of film.

We also had perhaps the most vital environmental rule of all: parents who gave us the opportunity to draw, free from excessive criticism, and free from excessive praise—Mother, because she felt that children in the exploration of life could do no wrong, and Father, I thought at the time, because he only wanted to get rid of that paper as soon as possible.

To this day, because this rule led us all into the wonderful world of drawing, I believe implicitly in these conditions. I believe that all children will learn the joy of drawing if encouraged by ample materials, and love strong enough from their parents—and it must be very strong—to refrain from the well-intended but deadly use of unqualified criticism or excessive praise during the very early, very critical, very creative years of childhood.

It is a happy experience to draw for the joy of drawing, not as a competitive exercise for parental approval. And so, all of our family became drawing addicts and drew our way through childhood, puberty, and into adulthood, whatever that is, and the paths of all of us can be easily traced by the windrows of

Ross Holt and debonair friend, Mount Washington, 1926

50

spent drawings trailing away into our past.

Therefore, it was no discouraging surprise to me that my first instructor at Chouinard Art Institute, like Nicolaides at the Art Students League, greeted his beginning classes with the following grim edict: "All of you here have one hundred thousand bad drawings in you. The sooner you get rid of them, the better it will be for everyone."

This was not a discouraging statement to me, because I was already well into my third hundred thousand.

I did not go to Chouinard Art Institute in the hope of seeing naked models. I simply didn't believe that. It was impossible. Nobody got to see naked women. I had never seen a naked woman, and, in truth, I'd never hoped to see one. Purple cows, yes; naked women, no. For one thing, I could not believe that any woman would ever take off all her clothes. This was too far outside my view of the laws of probability. So, when I attended my first "life class" at Chouinard in a converted stable

Embryonic animator (third from left) at Chouinard Art Institute, 1929

51

MAGIC MIRROR ON THE WALL. WHO IS THE UGLIEST ONE OF ALL

behind the old Victorian house on West Seventh Street in Los Angeles, I put up my drawing board, got out my charcoal, sandpaper pad, chamois, and arranged them all neatly before me, and looked up at the model stand, and just as I expected, a fully gowned young woman walked out from the dressing room, sat decorously down, took off her slippers, stood up, and let her dressing gown slip down over her white body, and assumed a simple pose. Nothing happened to me! Nothing! There was no doubt about it. She was, as my envious high-school classmate had said, "bare-ass naked." Indeed she was, including nipples, pubic hair, and all, and she stirred my stunned libido not one whit. My leering high-school associate had told me buttons would pop off my fly at first glimpse of a naked—they knew not the word "nude"—model. But this, to my utmost surprise, was not a naked woman but a nude model; she was there to be drawn. I was there to draw.

It was only later that I had a chance to contemplate the incongruity of the matter. And this only because, during a rest period in a late-spring semester, a lovely seventeen-year-old student sat down on the grass near me and her dress pulled up slightly over her rolled-up stocking, revealing perhaps an inch of creamy white, naked thigh. My high-school associate's predictions immediately came true: no buttons were lost, but I had to linger on the grass, thinking pure thoughts, before I could properly reenter the studio—after everyone else had gone in to calmly and unemotionally make a charcoal sketch of a nude model.

Chouinard in Los Angeles offered excellent schooling in the fine arts—painting and drawing in the classic traditions. But the most important and stunning discovery I made at Chouinard, one that has been shared by every artist, cartoonist, painter in history, from Cro-Magnon art to Claes Oldenburg by way of Leonardo, Goya, Frans Hals, Van Gogh, Herblock, and Beatrix

SL

SLAP

If a witch, in trying "to worm all her uglifying secrets" out of another witch, drinks "Acme Beautifying Potion" by mistake, horrifying and un-genie-ous things may occur: BROOMSTICK BUNNY (1956)

"BUT I JUST SAW A
GENIE WITH LIGHT
BROWN HAIR CHASIN'
A FLYIN' SORCERESS"

Potter, was the ability to live by the single line—that single honest delineation of the artist's intent. No shading, no multiple lines, no cross-hatching, no subterfuge. Just that line. Was it Feininger or Kandinsky who said, "My little dot goes for a walk"? Just so; every point on a line is of equal importance. That is rule 1 of all great drawing. There is no rule 2.

It could not have been planned, because Chouinard was a going concern long before the flowering of character animation in Southern California, but the curriculum at Chouinard could not have been more pertinently planned to provide the tools necessary for the development of future animators. One of the greatest teachers of figure drawing, the prime discipline required by the animator, was Donald Graham, who accomplished the necessarily impossible; he taught drawing without imposing his personal style of drawing on his students, as, for example, did George Bridgeman. But, just as Simon Nicolaides did at the Art Students League for generations of Eastern artists and illustrators, Don Graham taught artists what they had to know

for the future of animation. He showed us how to think drawing, not to emulate style, how to follow your natural bent with confidence.

Don Graham, who would go on to teach the philosophy of drawing and movement at Disney when the features were in production, had only two basic appraisals of a student's work. "Having problems?" he would ask, or "Looks like you're having fun." The second was the supreme apothegm, the supreme tribute, the ne plus ultra, because having fun with drawing meant that *something* was sinking in; the lessons were bearing fruit. I would rather hear Don Graham say, "Having fun?" than win an academic award. Years after his death, indeed to this day, when a drawing seems to be going right, I can hear his kindly voice: "Having fun?" Yes. Yes, indeed. If sainthood can be bestowed on a great teacher—and it should be—then the mantle should fall first on Don Graham, patron saint of animation.

No one at Chouinard was studying to be an animator, or a dress designer, or a motion-picture director, a watercolorist or an industrial designer. Yet out of the same courses in the same years at Chouinard came fashion and costume designers, industrial engineers, live-action directors and actors, book illustrators, and several of the most noted animators of all time. I think none of these students had any idea how they were to apply their knowledge in the practical world beyond art school, but—to this day—what basic schooling is appropriate for a budding animator is exactly the same as for those other crafts.

An animator's best friends are his doodles

We can teach an artist to animate; we cannot take the time or expend the effort to teach him to be an artist.

So I came out of art school during the Depression, dreaming the dreams that all worthy art students dream: that I would become an easel painter, consumptive and unrecognized, dying picturesquely at some incredible old age like thirty-seven, in a wonderfully shabby Paris garret with my painfully completed masterpiece on the easel beside me, a sort of male Camille.

"STEAL WOOL"

a LOONEY TUNE CARTOON
TECHNICOLOR ®

© 1957   WARNER BROS. PICTURES INC.

1957

The starving part was partially accurate. For a while I lived near the school in a rooming house. And one day, in a weak and hungry moment, my roommate and I succumbed to a bit of larceny. A greengrocer's truck had parked down the street and was left untended. We grabbed the first crate we could off the back. It turned out to be celery. For two days we ate nothing but celery and used up more calories chewing than we realized in energy. "Damn it," I said to my roommate. "What're we going to do? We can't starve!" "That's funny," he replied. "I thought we could."

Tedd Pierce and Mike Maltese were caricatured for castaways and supplied the voices, too (1943)

Upon being thrust rudely into a rude world, I found that it takes money to die poor, so my ambitions went necessarily from the impracticably sublime to the practically realistic. I couldn't even afford to be ridiculous: I had to get a job.

I had no technical skills; I could not letter or write billboards. After all, Chouinard Art Institute was a fine-arts academy, not a trade school. We were all contemptuous of trade schools— good God, they taught you a trade! I had no physical skills— Chouinard had no teams, no physical education. We were all contemptuous of the physical. This was not, thank God, we said, USC! The heaviest thing I had ever lifted was a 2B pencil; even a 3B seemed an imposition.

There was one self-skill I had reasonable confidence in. In my first year at Chouinard, before I faked my way into a scholarship, I worked as a janitor in some office buildings. In those quaint days an office was considered incomplete without a cuspidor—or spittoon, if you wish to be delicate—and I had weathered that year with the unpleasant job, among others, of emptying these untidy containers. I even earned the sobriquet "Admiral" from a jolly real-estate agent who chewed cigars (he didn't smoke them, he chewed them, and wetly deposited their flaky remains into the waiting cuspidor). "Admiral" was so uproariously funny to him that he so dubbed me not once but 825 times, by actual count, in front of his slimy peers. "Because," he said, "he handles the vessels."

So I had some experience in this exacting trade and hope ran high in the Jones family that the expense of three years in art school might not have been in vain if it prepared me for a job as a janitorial assistant.

Janitors in those days were not yet known as sanitary engineers. Few of them read Proust or played the blockflöte, and, if anything, they were downwardly mobile rather than upwardly so.

The important and vital factor here was that janitors were actually paid for janiting and therefore, since I was, as Daffy Duck would later say, "dethtitute," I was ready—no, I was eager—to become once again an admiral, even a vice admiral—a more accurate term, anyway.

So I seemed destined once again to join the bucket brigade, when the hand of my Guardian Angel in the form of an old Chouinard schoolmate (Fred Kopietz, later a fine animator at Disney) tapped me in a way that led to a life I could not have envisaged in my wildest dreams (and I had some wild ones). I couldn't believe it then and I have difficulty believing it now: someone was willing to pay me to do what I most wanted to do. Imagine that!

Having fun, Chahl?

Mike Maltese in a jovial mood

A Few Hours' Incursion Into A Rabbit Factory

(Circa 1946)

(LAPINII SCHLESINGERIUS/ SELZERIUM)

COMPAN-NEE----

The stimulus of the war had enormously quickened the tempo of the age. The dawn of a new spirit was rising in the land . . . It was time for recklessness and rapid change.

— DORIS KEARNS GOODWIN

Although Mrs. Goodwin was speaking of the War between the States, she accurately describes the post-World War II atmosphere at our studio.

These last eighteen or twenty years of the Warner Bros. Cartoons output have often been described as our Golden Age.* If so, we were blissfully and fortunately unaware of it. What we rather wanly hoped was that our cartoons would have

A rabbit's occupation is determined by his headwear: BUGS BONNETS (1956)

* There is often talk of the Golden Age of animated cartoon short subjects. There were actually two. The first was the great years of the Disney shorts, beginning in 1933 with The Three Little Pigs and continuing through 1939. Nearly all the great writers, directors, and animators of that period went on to features such as Snow White. Our period of most effective production was lit by the spark of A Wild Hare in 1940. The full fruition was evident in the postwar period, 1945 to 1963. We would have been properly embarrassed by the term "Golden Age." To paraphrase George Sterling: "He only in a Golden Age lives who knows not he is there."

"Atten-shun!"

a life expectancy of four or five years, because in those simple yet wonderfully creative years *before* television, we made films solely for theatrical release. Indeed, *all* the cartoons now shown on television as the Bugs Bunny/Road Runner shows, etc., were made for that purpose.

We were not allowed to preview our films, nor thankfully were there any such idiocies as demographics or Nielsen ratings. Just like Chaplin, Keaton, and Lloyd before us, we made films without any knowledge of or desire to know the human composition of our audiences.

Like our distinguished forebears, we made pictures for ourselves, believing with childlike innocence that if we laughed at and with each other, others perhaps would follow.

As was once pointed out, money cannot buy poverty, and money unfortunately cannot buy laughter either. At least at Warner Bros. Cartoons, no effort was exerted to do so. We were grotesquely underpaid, but we were being paid to do what we enjoyed doing. We were being paid to associate *every* day with people we loved and respected, people who were eager, excited, and joyfully willing to try almost anything.

The peculiarly wild, unbridled quality of the studio of that day was not confined to the animation stage—laughter is catching and extended clear to the front desk, where Ginger Morgan, our freckle-nosed, redhead receptionist, happily transposed Schlesinger Productions into an exalted, inadvertent (she said) spooncrism, Pleasanter Seductions, when answering the telephone.

If you entered the front door on Van Ness Avenue at 9:30 a.m. of this day, you might well have found yourself gently shouldered aside by a blond young man burdened by a 25-pound chunk of ice and a huge picnic basket, who enters the reception booth, kisses Ginger Morgan on the back of her neck, and addresses a small mirror on the wall, "If you see Cal Howard, tell him I want to see him immediately," and tiptoes off down the hall. He is wearing one tennis shoe and one patent-leather pump.

"That's Cal Howard," Ginger says.

Ah, yes. Cal Howard. Cal Howard, writer, gagman, entrepreneur, and master of the unofficial Schlesinger Commissary.

Cal Howard's Hot Dog Stand.

Mr. Howard's boundless energy could never have been contained by a single job: if he had been a novelist during Prohi-

Christmas party, Leon Schlesinger studio, 1934(?); 3.2 beer had just become legal, hence the suds

bition, he would most certainly have run a speakeasy as the kind of calisthenic necessary to harness that energy. It was not so much a matter of extra money (although he never disdained pelf) as it was the joy of running a complete short-order diner under the ignorant nose of his superiors—a challenge too great to ignore for one of the most actively fecund minds of the Warner years.

Starting with the fundamental tools of the writer—chairs, desk, bulletin board—Mr. Howard's ingenuity converted his office into all the habiliments of a modern major bistro. His desk is a marvel of efficiency. All drawers are lined with zinc. One contains chopped ice, Coca-Cola, sacramental and Mogen David wines, Dr. Brown's celery tonic, etc.; another, a spice-and-mustard cupboard including condiments, condoms, and explosives; another contains dishes, napery, cutlery; another, a wired warming oven for breadstuffs, cookies, bagels, and lasagna; the typewriter well houses a small efficiency electric stove.

All this is hidden within the desk itself, and at the advent of an enemy, only the price list on the wall need be reversed to a tasteful picture of Our Lord, signed "To my pal, Cal, from Jesus." All other gastronomic equipment can be easily and quickly concealed simply by slamming the drawers.

And Mr. Howard need not attract a crowd to his bistro to function efficiently. A basket can be lowered from the upper floors by the attic-bound who are in need of nourishment. Cal points to the window: "Money comes down in a basket, provender goes up in the returning basket, simply a case of supply and demand. Basic stuff. But," he adds darkly, "constant vigilance is the key to success in this exacting business." There *had* been hijackings: two laden baskets *had* been diverted from their honest destinations by long metal hooks extended from adjoining windows.

Cal soon discouraged the raping of his baskets by switching a cargo that might be hijacked to one loaded solely with a lighted firecracker (truth being stranger than animation).

The only time Ray Katz, the studio's slue-footed business manager, ever came remotely close to discovering Cal's other life was when he entered his office one day just in time to see the upstairs basket being lowered outside the window.

Mr. Katz, whose intellect was far, far below that of sphagnum moss (more on that charming vegetable later), nevertheless was aware that baskets outside windows were something different, therefore suspicious. No doubt he had seen baskets before, or at least heard of them. Windows were old stuff, he'd *seen* windows. But baskets *and* windows together were quite possibly illegal. He pushed his fat blue head out the window to inspect the offending basket, fixed a pop-eyed glare at its contents: sixty cents in honest coin intended for the honest purchase of two hot dogs, two Cokes, and two aspirins. Mr. Katz, left to his druthers, would no doubt have been inclined to grab the money and run, hadn't sterner duties prevailed. "Uh?" he asked. A long speech for Mr. Katz.

Wile E. Coyote at his wiliest: READY, SET, ZOOM! *(1955)*

64

Cal Howard glanced up inquiringly from his diligently story-sketching fingers. "Ah, yes," he said, "a small contribution for my son's bar mitzvah." Cal was an unmarried Gentile.

Mr. Katz reared back on his fat feet. One thing one did not do is fool around with bar mitzvahs . . . Yahweh might be watching. Giving Cal an "Uh" of understanding and backtracking on crepe-lined shoes, he retreated to the safe harbor of his hidey-hole.

Inconsistency is the handmaiden of artistry, and the Warner Bros. directors, animators, and writers were indeed a laboratory for creative inconsistency, for unanticipated mutations, for happy accidents—a primal soup to discover the delight of the undiscovered. A place ideal for this ill-paid, enthusiastic, frolicsome group. Yes, a group never gathered before or since: how lucky we were.

Coyote demonstrating self-destructive ingenuity

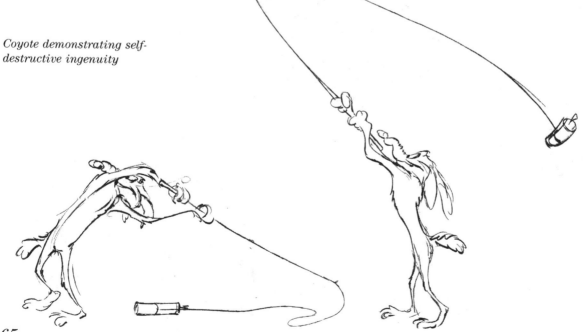

Hung-over rabbit after mixing carrot and turnip juice

Elmer Wait was a fine young assistant animator who died very young, a lost talent who deserves some recognition, so I will say only that Elmer Wait couldn't sleep at work. Insomnia is the most debilitating of all disorders, but to the young minds of young animators, almost any misfortune can, if carefully analyzed, be put to some use in the war with the front office. Wakefulness by itself is a hindrance rather than an advantage, but was it possible that there were other unexplored latent uses that could be tandemly harnessed to Elmer Wait's insomnia that would serve for the good of all? Indeed there were: Smokey Garner, the dear Swamp Rabbit of sainted memory and equal genius, had among his many talents the necessary ability to weave tiny invisible wires through the cobwebbed metal rafters descending from the ceilings of our dusty habitat.

The command post was at Elmer Wait's desk, which fortunately was in the first cubicle to be passed by intruders from

McGrew's pseudobiblical lament, 1939

Jones is my shepherd and I shall want. He maketh me to lie down with a headache. He leadeth me in deep water, He destroyeth my soul. He leadeth me in the paths of confusion for this names' sake. Yea, though I walk through the valley of the schedule of Leon, I shall fear no evil. Thy rod and thy stuff, they frighten me. Thou preparest a layout before me in the presence of mine enemies. Surely Jones and his schedule shall follow me all of the days of my life and I will dwell in the state institution forever.

66

the front office on their nefarious and intrusive incursions into our sacred domain.

Elmer Wait's eyes would have done credit to a rattlesnake; he could detect a movement so slight that it might be the nervous tic on a butterfly's face, and so Ray Katz, even though he wore gum shoes, was clearly mismatched in evading Elmer's lightning-like peripheral vision.

Mr. Katz never was able to associate Elmer's oily-tempered blue-steel eyes with his, Ray Katz's, inability to ever catch any animator sleeping, loafing, daydreaming, or doing anything but working. The one thing that was clear to Mr. Katz was that animators *should* be drawing. What they should be drawing he did not know, but draw they must or he would know the reason why. Even the term "drawing" was a little obscure to Ray Katz, who once commented on a director's observation that the brilliant designer John McGrew "can certainly draw, can't he?" Mr. Katz would have none of this nonsense: "Of course he can draw; he's an artist, isn't he?"

So Mr. Katz knew not that Elmer Wait's eye and Elmer Wait's thumb were connected, or that when he, Mr. Katz, passed Elmer Wait's doorway (there was no door—in Mr. Katz's philosophy, privacy leads to trouble, as has been proven by the fat brains of fat brass in lavatories of any army camp), so, as Mr. Katz, like Pippa, passed Elmer Wait's cubicle, Elmer Wait's thumb would press a small red button under the angle of his drawing board and small red lights would pop on all over the studio, tucked under the lowest shelves of the drawing-and-animation boards of every animator, layout man, background man, director, and writer; and every animator, background man, layout man, director, and writer would either awaken or be shaken awake by an alert young associate, and any sign of lethargy was immediately dispelled, to be replaced by an entire staff drawing at such a breakneck pace they could

John McGrew

67

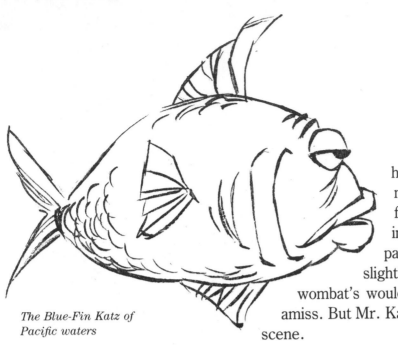

The Blue-Fin Katz of Pacific waters

have completed an entire animated cartoon in one day. This frenetic appearance, so endearing to the front office, was so patently false that an intellect only slightly more spry than a retarded wombat's would have realized something was amiss. But Mr. Katz took only joy in this spurious scene.

A more observant executive in another studio had once noted that an animator who had been sleeping face-down on his peg-studded drawing board might appear to be working diligently but the two or three small red spots on his forehead indicated that he had certainly been sleeping only a few moments before. Not that we expected such deductive abilities from Mr. Katz, but just to be safe, doctoring those spots with a little panchromatic makeup was considered good form.

The euphoric placidity enjoyed by Mr. Katz at the sight of his industrious animators was soon shattered on his next stop by the scene that met his eyes, creating a puzzlement that he carried to his grave. This stop was at one of the large story rooms, where most of the writers and directors had immediately congregated at the tocsin call of the early warning system. If his knowledge of the duty of an animator was abysmal, his knowledge of what went on in the directional division was, on a scale of one to ten, a minus one. A sluggish slug would soon have discerned what escaped Ray Katz: writers and directors wrote and directed animated cartoons by the development of storyboards, very similar to gigantic Sunday comic strips—one hundred fifty 3 × 5 inch sketches thumbtacked to a framed 4 × 8 foot storyboard. It *was* somewhat difficult to grasp the fact that animation writers do not write but draw, and animation directors do direct but draw also. The only thing that Ray could

Real Jones, 1941

gather from all this was that "lotsa" drawings were "good" and that no drawings at all were—as another intellect by the name of Slapsie Maxie Rosenbloom once said upon noticing his first solar eclipse: "Gee, dat's bad, ain't it?"

So when, rich in the production euphoria of his view of his industrious animation staff, he burst into the story room expecting live energetic action, poor Ray Katz never, never in all those years found a writer or director working. Since he didn't know what we were supposed to be doing, he had no way of criticizing us for not doing it.

We had been doing work, of course, before the little red lights went on. But our energetic love for what we did we were reluctant to demonstrate in the face of the enemy. So the scene that invariably greeted the bulging eyes of Mr. Katz was always the same: one of us would be reading a newspaper, another

Fake Jones, 1941

*Visual comments by Bob
Clampett*

energetically shining his shoes, another lazily drinking a Coke, another sleeping and making little whimpering sounds to prove it, and finally—aha!—one of us would actually be writing. However, he would stop at the advent of Mr. Katz, crumple up the paper, toss it in a desultory way into the wastepaper basket, and pick up the racing form. But the horror of the matter was that the storyboard was empty. Mr. Katz would then indulge in his only form of communication: rocking back and forth on his heels and toes and clucking like a hen. Whereupon everyone in the room would cluck back. In the face of this never-anticipated response, Mr. Katz would beat a hasty retreat, inadvertently triggering the "off" button in Elmer Wait's cubicle as he passed to his sanctuary.

Several hours later his door would slide silently open and he would tiptoe down the hall—red alert!—to find again his little elves hammering out drawings like the little machines he supposed them to be—and once again Mr. Katz would be completely unprepared for the dreadful experience in the story room: Mr. Katz would open the door and find the *same* person who two hours before had been shining his shoes still shining his shoes, the *same* person drinking the same Coke, the *same* person reading the *same* page of the *same* newspaper, and so on. A tableau of sameness, with one small altered detail: there were now forty or fifty sketches firmly pinned to the storyboard. If you have ever heard a six-foot blue chicken cluck in bewilderment, you will need no further explanation from me, but it may be that you have never heard five or six animation directors and writers sympathetically cluck back in response. I can tell you: *that*, my dears, is great music.

Those little dancing stick figures that most children learn to draw on the corners of tablets or textbooks are the essential tools of animation. The flipping of them into a gyrating frenzy is a precise parallel to putting them sequentially under a camera

Hijinks: HIGH NOTE (1960)

and, in essence, flipping them through a projector to a screen for the observation of larger audiences.

Anyone but Ray Katz would gather then that flipping a sheaf of drawings is the classic test for the animator. Having completed a series of drawings for a given piece of action, before the in-between drawings are added, the animator becomes his own test camera by flipping his drawings, just as he did in grammar school. However, this constant and repetitive flipping by every member of every unit, sixty or seventy people, continued to be a mystery, a puzzlement, an enigma to Mr. Katz.

Eighteen years of observation eventually bore fruit: Mr. Katz decided to avoid licking this whole matter of flipping by joining it. He, too, would flip.

No sooner said than done. One fine memorable morning, with the enormous confidence born of sheer ignorance, he strode into the music room, where two directors and story men had joined our composer Carl Stalling to go over the score of a soon-to-be-recorded film. The music score of this film, thirty

Left to right, standing: (?) Jones (unrelated), John McGrew, Bob Givens, Richard Kent Jones (related), C. Jones, Alex Ignatiev, Roy Laufenburger, Rich Hogan, Ken Harris, Phil Monroe; in front: Jack Phillips, Bobe Cannon, unidentified, Phil DeLara, Rudy Larriva, Ben Washam, Paul Julian (1940)

or forty pages of bar sheets, rested comfortably on the desk top as Ray Katz walked in, determined to become one of the boys; if they could flip, he could flip. Casually he picked up the unoffending music score and, under the fascinated and glazed gaze of those present, moved to the window for better light and carefully flipped the music score two or three times. Then nodding and grunting his appreciation of the artistry therein, departed, clucking to the group on his way out. The term "dumbfounded" found new meaning that day, as did "delight."

And that is how it came about that every succeeding music score was presented to Mr. Katz to be flipped for his endorsement and his professional and artistic approval.

Another strange and wonderful denizen of our sacred halls was the patrician Edward Stacey Pierce III, as different from writer Cal Howard as Groucho Marx was from Harpo. If Edward Stacey Pierce (sometimes known as Tedd Pierce—with two "d"s) were to conduct a tour of the studio, it might have gone something like this:

"Here," says Mr. Pierce III, taking your arm and entering a dark tunnel, "is the alimentary canal of this rabbit factory. On the right is the ink-and-paint department, peopled by a gathering of females unique in the world, topped only by the gin-alley sequence from Hogarth's *The Rake's Progress*. It is overseen by Florence Finklehor. Out of these portals each week pour four to five thousand inked and painted 'cels'—short for celluloids—ready to be gobbled up by the adjoining camera room. The camera crane upon which the camera sits is, *aptly enough*, an Acme, since every bit of hardware from an egg crate to a factory was always Acme. On the left side of this miserable hall is the larger sweatbox known as the projection room. As we enter this torture chamber you will note that the rabble sits in decayed church pews pirated from some decayed Warner feature, *Our Dancing Dung Beetles* or some such. At the back of this peeling parody of an auditorium you will note a golden throne, flaking and eczema-like to be sure, but nevertheless the haughty seat of our dauntless leader: Leon Schlesinger the Unready, or Leon the Unreasonable, or Leon the Unbearable, take your choice; any word starting with 'un' will fit Leon. This throne once enjoyed the pressure of the beautiful bottom of Nita Naldi in the first *Ten Commandments*, perhaps. It could even have been the fulsome buns of Norma Talmadge or perhaps Theda Bara (Arab spelled backwards), bottoms far, far more appealing than that of the ass who occupies it now."

"Is the studio contemplating an animated feature?" one might ask.

Leon Schlesinger, with unknown object in right foreground

Tedd's reply: "Mr. Schlesinger's initial response on seeing *Snow White* was delivered with his usual amazing grace: 'I need a feature cartoon like I need two assholes.'"

On the next door, beneath the word *Men*, someone has written:

LES PECKERAYS DE CAVALIERS RELIEVES VOUS
DANS CETTE ROOM

"Mike Maltese's Pepé Le Pew fractured French," Tedd might say. "It can be found throughout this theater of delights."

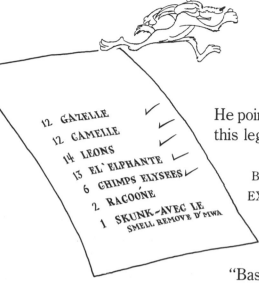

12 GAZELLE ✓
12 CAMELLE ✓
14 LEONS ✓
13 EL'ELPHANTE ✓
6 CHIMPS ELYSEES ✓
2 RACOONE
1 SKUNK~AVEC LE
SMELL REMOVE D'MWA

"Le Français fractured"

He points across the hall. Across the way, another door displays this legend:

BEYONDEZ-VOUS CETTE DOOR EST LE BOX-D-SWEAT
EXISTEZ ICI BEAUCOUP DE FILME-FLAMABLEZ-MUCHO
DOWZEZ-VOUX TOUTE DE CIGARETTES BEFOREZ
VOUS ENTREZ, SILVER PLATE

"Basically," says Mr. Pierce admiringly, "it means 'No Smoking.' The sign on the ladies' room upstairs more simply states:

"LA BELLE FEMME PUSSÉ RECLINEAU DANS CETTE ROOM."

"Does everyone around here speak like Pepé Le Pew?" you ask.

"One nice thing about Pepé Le Pewese is it confuses management." It is obvious that Mr. Pierce considers anything that confuses management automatically justified.

A pink guardsman's mustache dominates the face of another young man hanging his body half out of a doorway and extending a handsome watercolor: "Would you say there is an ineluctable modality to these nimbi?"

"If you mean clouds, why don't you say clouds?" says Pierce III. "You've been reading too much Joyce. Paul Julian, background artist or layout man. These strange creatures are a breed apart. This one also speaks Gaelic"—pause—"but with such a strong Erse accent that you can hardly understand him. On the left again, the murky habitat of Smokey, also known as Swamp Rabbit, aka Henry Garner, our test cameraman. The genius with the wonderful green thumbs of the inspired mechanic."

Farther on the left, through an open door, a dark-haired young man can be seen furiously pursuing a fly with a rapier.

"As you can see—a different breed," Mr. Pierce III points out. "Old Bob Holdeman here, one of our layout men, once bisected a live light cord with that sword, improved the speed of his background output for several hours."

A huge room is to the right, lined by a series of walled cubicles, each containing two desks, the backs facing outward, concealing the activities, illicit or otherwise, of the inhabitants.

"This is Chuck Jones's animation unit, sometimes called Unit A," says Mr. Pierce III. "Animators and in-betweeners live here. 'In-betweener' is an esoteric term for those who insert drawings between the animator's drawings, which in turn are known as 'extremes.' "

"Charlie. Dog. Easy!" an anonymous voice calls from behind one of the cubicles.

Unit A's Christmas card to C.J., 1940—left to right, back row: Ken Harris, Keith Darling, Bob Givens, Ace Gamer, Richard Kent Jones, Alex Ignatiev, unknown (but a good caricature!); center row: Phil DeLara, Rich Hogan, Bob McKimson, John McGrew, Phil Monroe, Roy Laufenburger, Steve Milliman; front row: Dave Monahan, Paul Julian, Rudy Larriva, Bobe Cannon, unknown (looks like Ronald Reagan; seems unlikely), Ben Washam

76

Thornton (Tee) Hee, great caricaturist; later sylphlike. Describable at this time (1941) as "a hot water bottle full of Jell-O"

"Submarine! You bastard, you got my submarine!" another anonymous voice indignantly answers.

"It's a game called Battleship," says Mr. Pierce III. "Keeps the natives amused in the early hours. Ever since management in its idiotic wisdom installed a time clock, no one works between eight and ten in the morning. Before the hated time clock was installed, everyone reported in at 9:00 a.m. and went right to work. No more. That clock is indeed a one-armed bandit, contradicting its very reason for being installed in the first place. By insulting the help with that cyclopean tyrant, management now loses about a hundred man-hours a day. Writers are exempt, of course—even management recognizing that no writer would have the strength to pull the arm of that digital indignity.

"There are usually three units like this—each composed of four or five animators, five or six in-betweeners, a layout man, and a background man. I doubt if any of them are working now, it's only 9:45. Perhaps it would be well for me to set a good example by taking my pre-tiffin nap now. Adieu." And Mr. Pierce dissolves into the woodwork.

It isn't every studio that has a cameraman who once traveled a backwoods vaudeville circuit with a seal named Eunice. Our studio did. He was one of our proudest possessions. His name was variously Smoke House, Swamp Rabbit, Smokey Hank, or for short, Henry Garner. Although almost illiterate, he was a mechanical genius. It never occurred to him that you had to know the theory behind anything to make it work. It was supposed to function ("sposed to fiction"), so he would fix it; he once corrected a malfunction of the worm gear on our Acme camera crane with a beer-can opener, a patently impossible thing to do. Smokey used a beer-can opener the way an engineer uses a slide rule. If a problem couldn't be solved with a beer-can opener, why, it couldn't be solved at all—better buy a new whatever-it-is. Nothing mechanical at our studio ever

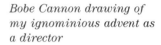

Bobe Cannon drawing of my ignominious advent as a director

went unsolved. Smokey would shuffle in (he never saw the sense in lifting his feet when he could slide them), move in on the problem (which could be anything from a recalcitrant electric eggbeater used in the ink-and-paint department to a hideously jammed ribbon-snarled typewriter), and fix it.

Our producer, Leon Schlesinger, once ordered Smokey to fix his constipated Cadillac. It took Smokey Garner ten minutes to slither the necessary fifty yards and thirty seconds to get that huge eight-cylinder machine purring. In this case he used a small piece of baling wire and a Good Humor ice-cream stick.

As John Steinbeck pointed out, there is no name for a "green thumb" in mechanics, but that is precisely what Smokey had, and Mr. Schlesinger showed his appreciation of his genius by paying him $16 a week. Aside from the two production camera cranes, there was nothing in the entire Schlesinger studio that had any value at all except Schlesinger's richly caparisoned front office. Leon did not believe in spending money, and Smokey's work area was clear evidence of that reluctance. Mr. Garner was in charge of shooting pencil tests, splicing them into loops to be studied, and then running them in the projection test room (or sweatbox); manning the ancient Cooper-Hewitt projector in the big projection room, keeping that monster and every

other decrepit thing in the studio running. Maybe he was paid $18 a week. I know he once asked Mr. Katz, our business manager, for a "crease in his celery." Mr. Katz professed not to understand what he was talking about, but Mr. Katz never understood what anybody was talking about when the delicate subject of salary increases was on the docket.

Smokey's camera stand was made of two-by-fours mounting a 1912 Bell & Howell camera made of brass and cherrywood, looking very much like the case that microscope slides would have been carried in by Oliver Wendell Holmes the Elder. Smokey built the stand himself, and it worked better and more efficiently than did the $40,000 production stands. He built his film dryer out of three bicycle wheels and some slats from a purloined rabbit hutch. The test projector was so old and odd-looking that no one had known it was a projector—and maybe it wasn't, but Smokey Garner used it as one; so if the name of an object is determined by its function, then this gear-cluttered telegraphic-looking object was a motion-picture projector.

But with all his other skills, Henry Garner's greatest joy for us was his wondrous disregard of the precision of the English tongue. In his short life, had he passed through academia, he would have left linguists swooning in phonemic horror in his wake. The difficulty of our language was his playground. If a word or a name was too intricate for easy phrasing, he simply adjusted it to a pleasanter and more convenient one: "Schlesinger" became the much smoother "Slesser." "Tiger" became "tagah." "Accidental collage" naturally follows—whoever heard of "Occidental"? Sounds more like an orthodontist's mistake. The "tagah," or "tiger," is indeed "Accidental's" symbol; "simple" is much smoother, but just in case you have doubts about "simple," Smokey would add an etymological simplifier. One of the loveliest of all his contributions to an often sterile language: "Accidental's enema."

Smokey Garner, the
brilliant Swamp Rabbit

79

It took weeks for us to make the quantum leap from "enema" to "emblem." We treasured Smokey far too much to ever think of correcting him; one would as soon scratch in a cathedral. All languages have music, and Smokey's was no exception. We respected his adjusting English to his own melodic principles, and if we did not always understand him immediately, the translation was worth the wait.

His lexicographic adjustments were so subtle at times that often we missed them altogether or subconsciously adopted them into our own vocabulary without knowing we were doing so. I used the term "flat-rock rifle" for years before realizing that "flint-lock" was what I had in mind. Curiously, I translated "raffle" to "rifle" without disturbing "flat rock." Friz Freleng got "wireless terrier" from Smokey. Bob McKimson used "fireman red" and "cold water heater," the latter I suppose because of its accuracy—"hot water heater" is redundant and silly; "cold water heater" makes sense.

Just before alcoholism killed Smokey Garner, he committed himself to a state institution at Oxnard, California. Upon his return we naturally asked what it was like up there. "Too hot," he said. "They had me in the spaggers."

This seemed to me very cruel punishment to inflict on a man who, after all, was suffering a terrible disease. Where were the spaggers, and why was it hot in the spaggers? Were the spaggers small concrete-and-iron punishment boxes broiling in the sun? Were the spaggers some sort of esoteric red-hot pliers? There was no point in looking in the dictionary for clues; we had exhausted that possibility years ago and we were honor-bound not to disturb the fragility of the matter by asking Smokey for precise elucidation; so it was only an overheard conversation just before Smokey went to his appointment in Samarra with a broken stair-riser and a cement sidewalk that I understood. "It was awful hot out in the sun under the tocas-blue sky, working

Frustratus lupus

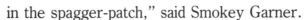

in the spagger-patch," said Smokey Garner.

Which leads me to another remarkable man I once misunderstood and now understand too well.

I have kept many things for their sentimental value—often things from people toward whom I have no sentimental attachments—but for the objects themselves that seem to me to be sentimental in nature and therefore treasurable. Russell Jones gave me what he could—and I valued his gift for many years without knowing exactly why, subconsciously moved by it, I suppose, and finally misplacing it, to my sorrow. The gift was a large clean mayonnaise jar containing three rubber-banded bunches of Good Humor ice-cream sticks, stained with marks of ancient and synthetic cherry and chocolate and Neapolitan dyes and sugars. These, too, had been scrubbed and washed

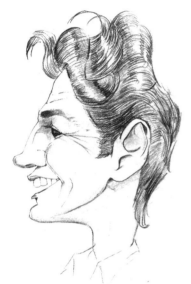

Smokey

Background from ONE
FROGGY EVENING (1955)

81

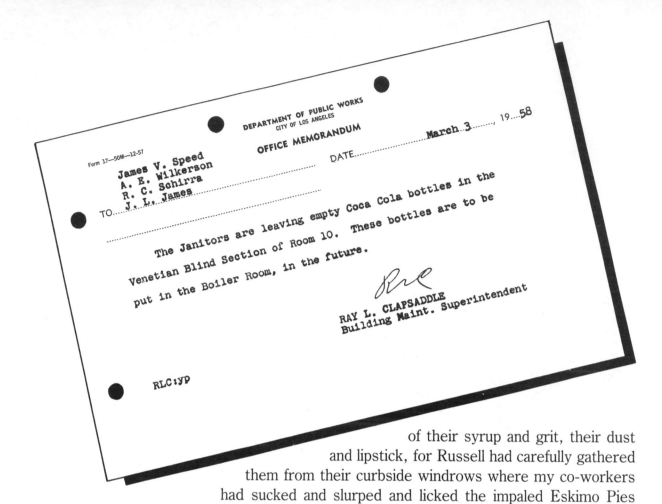

DEPARTMENT OF PUBLIC WORKS
CITY OF LOS ANGELES

OFFICE MEMORANDUM

DATE................March 3........, 19...58

James V. Speed
A. E. Wilkerson
R. C. Schirra
TO......J. L. James

The Janitors are leaving empty Coca Cola bottles in the Venetian Blind Section of Room 10. These bottles are to be put in the Boiler Room, in the future.

RAY L. CLAPSADDLE
Building Maint. Superintendent

RLC:yp

Bureaucracy is stranger than fiction

of their syrup and grit, their dust and lipstick, for Russell had carefully gathered them from their curbside windrows where my co-workers had sucked and slurped and licked the impaled Eskimo Pies during their three-o'clock break.

Russell had found me one night at work stirring a small pot of poster paint with a tongue depressor rescued from my infant daughter's collection of medical gear. It seemed an ideal paint paddle, as I pointed out to Russell when he entered my office, using his broom, as he always did, as a cane rather than a brush, to help support his arthritic hips. On nights when I worked late, he was my confidant, my friend, my philosopher. I cared for him, but I had no idea how much he cared for me.

Russell was far too old, far too bent, far too gnarled for his sixty years; he was not a very good janitor, and his territory was vastly overextended. It was an old building, more of a loft, a moldy beehive, dry and dusty. Dirt and waste could hardly be removed, so Russell's way was to stir it about, redistribute it, rearrange the patterns in mysterious halting ways of his own. Forty-five minutes of his every night were spent napping on the private toilet of our producer, who believed this plumbing

to be sacrosanct to his sacred frog-belly white buttocks. The needs of nature Russell answered were never physical, the elderly building was never shaken nocturnally by the pompous gush of its only truly modern piece of plumbing. It was rather, I think, Russell's quiet contribution to the studio-wide contempt and studio-wide rebellion against the toilet's proprietor, who badgered waiters, women, and Russell Jones, because they were helpless in the face of economic threats that floated always on the surface of our producer's pale eyes. Yet this nocturnal sedentary gesture was Russell's only rebellion and, to the studio personnel, the only gift he could afford. And we loved him for it.

It is twenty years too late for me to tell Russell Jones that I know now the value of his gift: that those scrubbed and stained bundles of confectionery sticks in their clean jar were the best that Russell could do for me; and because in all tasks his pain-ridden body forced him to do one at a time, I know each stick he rescued meant that he must painfully bend over again and again for me, and I know too well from watching him work how difficult this was and how reluctantly he had to set his twisted brown feet for any bending action, and yet he *did* bend a hundred times or more to provide the only gift he could provide and he knew I needed.

Russell Jones at work

STUDIO CLOSED
ON ACCOUNT
OF STRIKE

*The six-day war at the
Schlesinger studio, May 1941*

We are having a two-way motorcade ~~tomorrow night~~ Thursday at the Disney Studio. We need a lot of cars to start at each end of Buena Vista and drive <u>slowly</u> back and forth in front of the entrance. If the departure of the non-strikers is somewhat hindered by this maneuver it will be too bad, of course.

Please sign this if you can be out there <u>with a car</u>. If you do not have acar <u>do not sign</u> but be sure to come out with some one who has.

Sign your name after a number. Odd numbers (1-3-5,etc) will meet at Riverside and Buena Vista. Even (2-4-6, etc) will meet at Alameda and Buena Vista.

5:15. Thursday, July 17th.

1. CHUCK JONES
2. John Mc Grew
3. Rudy Larriva
4. Roy Hartenberger
5. Liz Le Blanc
6. PHIL DoLARA
7. Alexander Ignatiev
8. KEN HARRIS.
9. Abe Levitow
10. R.F. CANNON.
11. R.K. JONES
12. Phil Monroe
13. HAL GODDARD
14. Ted Pierce.
15. GIBSON SIKO
16. GERRY CHINIQUY
17. RICH THOMPSON
18. Costa Lebudeff
19. Murray Hudson
20. KEITH DARLING
21. BOB MATZ
22. RUDY ZINGLER
23. ROSS
24. Louis Appet
25. Ben Shenkman
26. Dave Mitchell

Familiar names support the Disney strike that followed soon after the six-day war. A telegram from Dorothy Parker read: "It's time that Walt Disney decided whether he is a man or a mouse"

Photo: Schlesinger strike, May 1941

The Front Office

Elmer Fudd as the lisping giant in BEANSTALK BUNNY (1955)

Many of the producers of animated cartoons were just as ignorant, foolish, and dangerous as their counterparts in the feature division. From Fred Quimby at M-G-M, who admonished Tex Avery in the midst of the war to be circumspect in his caricature of Adolf Hitler in *The Blitz Wolf* ("After all, Tex, we don't know who's going to win the war"), to Leon Schlesinger at Warner Bros., whose lisped admonitions contained such jewels as: "Put in lottsa joketh, felleth, joketh are funny"; and after looking around at our shabby quarters, "I wouldn't work in a shit-hole like this."

Leon Schlesinger was a master of good taste who often bought a win ticket on every horse in every race at Santa Anita in order to demonstrate by flashing the winning tickets to his underlings his acumen and knowledge of horse flesh. Leon's sole method of determining the quality of an animated cartoon was how far it came in under budget.

Until he sold the studio in 1944 to Warner Bros., Leon Schlesinger had functioned as an independent producer, financing his productions and selling them to Warner Bros. After the sale was completed, Eddie Selzer was installed as producer by Jack Warner, following a diligent search of the studio to find out who hated laughter most. Eddie won, hands and dewlaps down.

Fifteen years after I started directing, Eddie inveigled a luncheon engagement for Friz Freleng, Bob McKimson, and

ACADEMY OF MOTION PICTURE ARTS AND SCIENCES
THE SHORT SUBJECTS BRANCH
PRESS PREVIEW
of new
OUTSTANDING SHORT SUBJECTS
(With emphasis on the War effort)

Wednesday Evening, August 19, 1942   **Filmarte Theatre, Hollywood**

1. **TERROR OF THE MIDWAY.** Paramount. It's SUPERMAN!—This time battling a giant gorilla in a burning circus. No. 9 in the series directed by Dave Fleischer.

2. **COMMUNITY WAR CHEST.** Produced by the Motion Picture Industry for the Community Chests and Councils of New York for national distribution. This trailer is an example of a peacetime public service by the ind___ adapted to present conditions. Together with a similar trailer, COMMU___ it will be used this Fall. Mark Sandrich, Director; Charles Lang___

3. **VICTORY VITTLES.** Metro-Goldwyn-Mayer. Wherein ___ commentator, Pete Smith, concocts an assortment of delectable ___ assistance of the popular home-economist, Polly Patterson. W___ in food preparation are stressed. Will Jason, Director. In Tec___

4. **THE DUCK-TATORS.** Leon Schlesinger-Warner B___ Schlesinger style concerning the iniquities of a bad egg___ gullible goose named Benito, and a sappy Jappy named H___ are thwarted by the dove of peace. Supervised by Norma___

5. **THE GREATEST GIFT.** Metro-Goldwyn-Mayer. A ___ featuring Edmund Gwenn, the story being based on an ___ an itinerant juggler who is befriended by a group of k___ Goldstone, Producer; Harold Daniels, Director.

6. **THE MAN ANGLE.** Paramount. Robert Benchle___ things that some women do that may cause a certain ___ man's life — not all women, of course, but these things a___ No. 5 in the Benchley series for Paramount.

7. **THE OLYMPIC CHAMP.** Walt Disney-RKO R___ very hard to illustrate in clear detail the various athle___ Olympic performer. Continuing the series which ha___ A HORSE, HOW TO SKI, and THE ART OF SELF-___

8. **PREPARATION OF A SAND TABLE.** An ___ duced by the Academy Research Council for the ___ be shown in theatres, but only to army personnel. ___ nearly 200 reels of such training films, which as___ in all branches of the service. This particular su___ training to instruct non-commissioned officers i___ tactical problems on a sand table.

9. **WOODMAN, SPARE THAT TREE.** Col___ crow is a match for a tree-chopping fox, and a___ Current release in the Color Rhapsody series. ___

10. **BEYOND THE LINE OF DUTY.** Prod___ only and not for public or theatrical release, t___ tary morale or war training type of film, w___ specific instructional films for technical traini___ the leading role—all the cast being army person___ tion equipment supplied by Warner Bros. The intent of the ___ the importance of the work performed by the Air Force flying instruct___ must give up a personal place in the fighter squadrons in order to train others. Produced by Gordon Hollingshead. Lewis Seiler, Director; narration by Lt. Ronald Regan.

11. **THE BLITZ WOLF.** Metro-Goldwyn-Mayer. A cartoon which traces the infamous tactics of a certain nefarious mustached character given to violent outbursts of rug-chewing. Fred Quimby, Executive Producer; Tex Avery, Director.

ACADEMY SHORT SUBJECTS REVIEW COMMITTEE—Pete Smith, Chairman, Jules White, Lewis Notarious, Milton Hoffman, Jack Cutting, James Simons, Will Cowan, Arnold Albert, John LeRoy Johnston, Arch Reeve, and Donald Gledhill.

Congratulatory message from Private Nelson Demorest, who was unfairly erudite

> Dear Chuck,
>
> New York
> Apr. 10, 38
>
> If you can win arguments from Demorest like you used to, its a cinch you can direct. Ask Clampett.
>
> Congratulations. Confidence and Luck
>
> Nelson
>
> 126 Hauxhurst
> Weehawken,
> New Jersey.
> (for next 5 weeks only)

Eddie Selzer in a jovial mood

The Great Friz Freleng . . .

the Great Tex Avery . . .

both of whom survived my services as an animator

me at the ornate private dining room where the brothers Warner and their minions would have a chance to patronize us in comfort. Harry Warner set the tone of our day in court by observing that he had no idea where our cartoon division was, and added, "The only thing I know is that we make Mickey Mouse." We were proud to hear that and assured him that we would continue to keep Mickey at the top of his popularity. Jack Warner suggested that it would be healthiest for our future if we did so.*

Friz Freleng contends that the Warner brothers implicitly believed we made Mickey Mouse, until 1963—when, shocked to discover that we did not, they shut the studio.

Leon had been, in contrast to Eddie, a real charmer, a sort of snazzily dressed Gila monster in a Panama hat, white flannel trousers, and black-and-white pointy shoes. He did, if memory serves, inadvertently contribute one of the most vital dramatic factors to our little company.

It was Tex Avery's duck that memorialized Leon Schlesinger. In Tex's *Porky's Duck Hunt*—the first Daffy Duck film (1937)—Daffy's voice was a sort of cross between a stuttering "hoo-hoo" and a spluttering laugh. Tex felt that "hoo-hoo"s could go stale with repetition and that there was a vital difference in a duck that was nutty and a duck that *enjoyed* being nutty. But he still needed a voice, and it was Cal Howard (whose claim to immortality was already well established by his subterranean hot-dog stand) who suggested that Leon Schlesinger's lisp plus Leon's absolute belief that the world owed him

* *As reported, a couple of years later Jack demonstrated his knowledge of the value of the cartoons by selling all the pre-'48 cartoons (probably four hundred of them) for $3,000 apiece. It is a matter of record that each of these four hundred cartoons has averaged over $5,000 a year in rentals alone.*

Anyone for Tennis!!

"Niceth Game!"

Daffy mistakenly asks Elmer Fudd for a bit of sport

DUCK! RABBIT! DUCK! (1953)

Bad Day?

Bill Scott as a social observer

90

a living made him a perfect prototype for Daffy. Mel Blanc saw no difficulty in marrying Leon's voice to a duck, so the deed was done, and Daffy found a new voice as well as a new personality, an acquisitiveness to match Leon's.

But all unbeknownst, and only when we were well into the production of the new film and incapable of retreat, did we realize the hideous, the lethal potential of the future: Leon Schlesinger was going to have to see this film, and—more important to our future—to hear his very own voice emanating from that duck.

In order to save ourselves the embarrassment of being fired, all of us were careful to write out our resignations before that fateful day when Leon strode into our projection room and sprawled on the gilt throne he had snatched from some early Warner pseudo-De Mille film or other. The rest of us, of course, still sat on beat-up splintery church pews from an early family film. The new Daffy Duck lit up the screen at Leon's courteous command: "Roll the garbage!" The cartoon played to the studio audience, accompanied mainly by crickets, prayers, and silence.

Then the lights went on and Leon leaped to his feet, glared around: "Jeethus Christh, that's a funny voithe! Where'd you get that voithe?"

So Leon went to his grave, his riches gone with Nineveh and Tyre, but wherever the voice of the turtle-duck is heard throughout the land, Leon is enshrined in the hearts of his countrymen.

Our long relationship with Leon Schlesinger many of us supposed was more than adequate preparation for any new producer we might face, yet we were hardly prepared for Eddie Selzer.

Once chosen by Jack Warner to head up the Warner Bros. newest acquisition, Eddie, in order to establish his vast knowledge of animation, demanded to see every script before it went into production, imitating his chieftain, Jack Warner. Jack always demanded scripts, though it was never proven that he could read. So Eddie demanded scripts, and in his twelve-year tenure it never became apparent to his mouse-like brain that there

Christmas party, Leon Schlesinger studio, 1935(?) —C. Jones buttering up both Ray Katz and Friz Freleng

Leon Schlesinger invites you to a Christmas Luncheon to be held on this lot Tuesday, December 24 at 12 Noon on stage 2

Kindly present this invitation at the stage entrance

Unit A, 1942—left to right, standing: Unknown (or at least unremembered), Eugene Fleury, Phil Monroe, Lloyd Vaughan, Rudy Larriva, Roger Daly, Cathy (later DeLara), Bobe Cannon, unknown (but well remembered), Roy Laufenburger; front row: C. Jones, Abe Levitow, Ben Washam, Tony Sgroi, Mike Maltese, unknown, Edward Stacey Pierce III, Phil DeLara, Richard Kent Jones, Ken Harris, Art Heineman

were no scripts for animated cartoons. (Eddie was a mouse studying to be a rat, according to Wilson Mizner, who also pointed out that Eddie never strayed from the straight and narrow-minded path.) So, for those twelve dreadful years of his reign, he demanded the impossible: the sort of man, said one writer, who makes his way through life like an untipped waiter.

Eddie, like the people in charge of network television today, hated and feared anything he had never seen before. Innovation, to him, was as a viper's fang, and he kicked and bucked at *every* innovative idea.

We became quickly aware of this endearing trait at his first showing of one of my cartoons at the studio. Eddie watched with baleful, unblinking eyes, making only one comment: "There's something new take it out." No comma after "new"; it actually sounded like "Theresomethinewtakitout"—one word. What he was criticizing was the kind of French spoken by Pepé Le Pew. "Nobody'd laugh at that shit" was his creative contribution to the showing.

His edicts, too, were very helpful: "I don't want any gags

about Ike." I'm sure this was a relief to Eisenhower, who no doubt lived in fear of our acerbic wit. Of course, Eddie hadn't noticed that we almost never included contemporary or temporal humor in our films.

Yet, although Eddie told me there was nothing funny about a skunk talking French and fought its use, he gracefully accepted as his right the Oscar when Pepé Le Pew won in 1950.

He once appeared in the doorway of our story room while Mike Maltese and I were grappling with a new story idea. Suddenly a furious dwarf stood in the doorway: "I don't want any gags about bullfights, bullfights aren't funny!" Exactly the words he had used to Friz Freleng about never using camels. Out of that dictum came *Sahara Hare*, one of the funniest cartoons ever made, with the funniest camel ever made.

Pepé in preliminary pose for "Strolling Through le Parque un Jour": WILD OVER YOU (1953)

Having issued his angry edict, Eddie stormed back to his office. Mike and I eyed one another in silent wonderment. "We've been missing something," Mike said. "I never knew there was anything funny about bullfighting until now. But Eddie's judgment is impeccable. He's never been right yet." "God moves in wondrous ways, his story ideas to beget," I replied.

Result: *Bully for Bugs*—one of the best Bugs Bunny cartoons our unit ever produced.

Perhaps his finest hour came at a story session.

Four or five of us were laughing over a storyboard when once again Eddie stood vibrating at the doorway, glaring malevolently at us and our pleasure and laughter. His tiny eyes steely as half-thawed oysters, his wattles trembling like those of a deflated sea cow. "Just what the hell," he demanded, "has all this laughter got to do with the making of animated cartoons?"

Bull sharpening his senses: BULLY FOR BUGS (1953)

In a lifetime search for a proper niche for producers on the ladder of living things, I was forced near the bottom to sphagnum moss, which seems to just sit there harmlessly, irritating no one, just quietly minding its own business. Obviously the producer, who might well be sued by poison oak in terms of irritability, belongs above sphagnum moss. A very short trip up the nether rungs of our ladder-of-life reveals the planarian worm. We must stop here, because the planarian worm seeks light, effectively putting it above the producers.

Nevertheless, our producers served an occasional purpose—inadvertent, as in the case of Leon Schlesinger and Daffy Duck. Intentional, as in the case of Eddie Selzer and *Bully for Bugs* and *Sahara Hare*. But perhaps their most valuable service to us was as someone to actively dislike; creativity without opposition is like playing polo without a horse. Contempt comes naturally when the artist is opposed by someone who can't write, draw, or laugh, and whose prime creative impulse is to say no. Fortunately for us, Leon Schlesinger was usually too lazy to even say no, but Eddie Selzer amply made up for this entrepreneurial deficiency. If Eddie was forced to reduce his entire vocabulary to one word, it would have been no contest—"no" would have won adverbially down. Anybody who hated camels, bullfights, and French-speaking skunks can't, I suppose, be all bad. As I look back, it seems to me that some of our best pictures emerged out of our constant fight against negativism. Aristotle, I think, wanted to be "a gadfly on the rump of the universe." Stimulating creativity is an admirable function. I suppose if the result is the same, the intentions of the fly are immaterial. So, even though I am reluctant to say it, Eddie Selzer, for all the wrong reasons, did all the right things to keep our creative nerves on edge and therefore active. If there is a puff adder loose in your house, you seldom get lazy.

BEEP, BEEP (1952)—we had to wait three years to do a second Road Runner film; management wasn't sure that this was a viable idea

*Bob Clampett's opinions of
Leon Schlesinger*

*Standing:
Treg Brown,
Bob McKimson,
C. Jones; seated:
Johnny Burton,
Eddie Selzer,
Friz Freleng*

*. . . and my view
of them in other
occupations*

THE DIRECTORS: FRIZ FRELENG, TEX AVERY, AND HOW I GREW

Friz Freleng

Tex Avery

. . . and Charles M. Jones—a dreadfully accurate portrait by a visiting Soviet cartoonist

"**Y**ou cannot imitate a master, but you are a fool if you ignore him."

It is difficult to be profound, analytical, or discerning about the art of Tex Avery, because profundity tends to interrupt laughter, and this is a poor trade indeed. Avery was a genius. As one of his animators in the later 1930s (at Warner Bros.), I was as ignorant of his genius as I suppose Michelangelo's apprentices were oblivious to the fact that they, too, were working with a genius. But Avery's brilliance penetrated the husk of my self-assured ignorance, the ignorance that encases most twenty-year-olds. In spite of myself, I learned from him the most important truth about animation: animation is the art of timing, a truth applicable as well to all comedy. And the most brilliant masters of timing were Keaton, Chaplin, Laurel and Hardy, Langdon—and Fred (Tex) Avery.

All the studios provided travelogues, apparently designed to give the theater audience a chance to go out and buy popcorn.* "Fitzpatrick Trave-

---

* *Years later Leonard Levinson, who owned Impossible Productions ("This is Impossible"), produced a travelogue about London, opening on a shot of the city as the fog came in, obliterating the entire screen. Against only this gray mass, the narrator commented for eight minutes on the wonders of the great capital.*

logues" became the generic name for all these films, just as, for many years, "Walt Disney" was the generic name for animation.

The "Fitzpatrick" technique pretty much ignored individuals; with voice-over only, the entire film could be shot with a silent camera. *Mysterious Cairo, Gay Rio de Janeiro* ("gay" in those days meant gay, not "gay"), *The Wonders of Sandusky, The Happy Zulus,* etc. Usually ending with "And so, as the sun sinks slowly in the west, we sadly say goodbye to beautiful Cairo, Rio, Sandusky, Zululand."

Tex went right for the jugular. In *The Isle of Pingo Pongo* he had a running gag of a little man (actually an ancestor of Elmer Fudd) named Egghead continually wandering through, carrying a violin case and interrupting the narrator, "Now, boss?" The narrator impatiently replies, *"No.* Not now!" And then embarrassedly carries on, until the end of the film, when

the sun is setting and the narrator sweetly says, "And so, as the sun sinks slowly in the west, we sadly say goodbye to the beautiful Isle of Pingo Pongo." The sun suddenly stops in mid-descent. The narrator impatiently repeats the whole line, "And so, as the sun sinks slowly in the west . . . ," but the sun refuses to cooperate. The narrator in more and more irritated tones repeats and repeats. No movement in the complacently stubborn sun.

Egghead walks in. "Now, boss?" "Yes!" screeches the narrator. "Now!"

Whereupon Egghead flips open the violin case, comes out with a rifle, and shoots the sun in its vitals, watching it plunge into the sea.

He ridiculed every platitude implicit in these cliché-ridden "educational" films: a lizard doing a striptease while shedding her skin; different sides of a split screen for grownups and children; and after a description with loving detail of the heating system and absolute cold impenetrability of the polar bear, the bear in question looks sadly at the audience: "I don't care what you say, I'm cold."

—And the echo from Mr. Fitzpatrick must have been: "I don't care what you say, *I'm* old hat."

Oh, lightning doesn't care where it strikes. But with Avery the lightning flashed in and out of the primal porridge of cute cartoons, sadly including early ones of mine, and out sprang a Crackpot Quail, a Haunted Mouse, a very, very Red Hot Riding Hood, a Satyr-Maniacal Wolf, a small Droopy, a canine cross between Muhammad Ali and Albert Einstein with a voice like a cooing dove. Dove? How about a 900-pound king-size canary? And the world's smallest half-pint pygmy?

What I learned during those early years from Tex, Friz Freleng, Mike Maltese, Tedd Pierce, and others, on my way to becoming a competent director, was this:

*Friz Freleng's sketch
reduces me to moccasins*

1. You must love what you caricature. You must not mock it—unless it is ridiculously self-important, like those solemn live-action travelogues.

2. You must learn to respect that golden atom, that single frame of action, that $\frac{1}{24}$ of a second, because the difference between lightning and the lightning bug may hinge on that single frame.

3. You must respect the impulsive thought and try to implement it. You cannot perform as a director by what you already know; you must depend on the flash of inspiration that you do not expect and do not already know.

4. You must remember always that only man, of all creatures, can blush, or needs to; that only man can laugh, or needs to; and that if you are in that trade of helping others to laugh and to survive by laughter, then you are privileged indeed.

5. Remember always that character is all that matters in the making of great comedians, in animation, and in live action.

6. Keep always in your mind, your heart, and your hand that timing is the essence, the spine, and the electrical magic of humor—and of animation.

Of course, never once did anyone hear words such as these from Tex Avery—he was not one to pontificate—but for all of us who worked with him and beside him the message was loud and clear; by his example he taught us. I would have imitated him, I suppose, if I had the remotest idea how to go about it, but since imitation of Tex Avery was impossible—others tried and fell short—I found to my pleasure and surprise that these rules applied equally well to all humor and all character animation. So there was plenty of room for me to seek my own way.

Joe Adamson in *Tex Avery, King of Car-*

CHUCK JONES

DIRECTOR
WARNER BROS. PICTURES, INC.
CARTOON DIVISION

THORNWALL 5-2633
RES. HOLLYWOOD 2-3915

Tex Avery's Bugs Bunny:
A WILD HARE (1940)

*toons,** probably brought the chubby will-o'-the-wisp named Tex into focus as well as anyone could, as difficult a task perhaps as Tex's instruction to an associate, after breaking wind: "Catch that one and paint it green." But Adamson came as close as possible: "Chuck Jones' coyote can fall five miles from a precipice and still be alive when he gets to the bottom. Tex Avery's wolf could probably endure such a fall but is more likely to develop brakes on the way down. It is the creation of the director's own universe, and the maintaining of that universe, that makes animation a medium capable of individual, personal expression, and what allows us to tell one animation director from another."

Tex Avery's could never be mistaken for anyone else's in animation. Consider: "Avery's films will roll along harmlessly enough, with an interesting situation treated in a more or less funny way. Then, all of a sudden, one of the characters will lose a leg and hop all over the place trying to find it again . . . In *Slap-Happy Lion*, a kangaroo hops into its own pocket and disappears. In *Billy Boy*, a goat is rocketed to the moon and eats it. In *Homesteader Droopy*, a pistol gets wounded in the midst of a gun battle and the owner must put it out of its misery."†

Tex, more than any other director, was fascinated by the limitless possible extensions of the medium. He simply ignored all the physical laws of the universe, with, perhaps, an occasional nod to the law of gravity.

As an animator I worked for both Tex and Friz Freleng for a couple of years each.

As a director I worked parallel to Friz Freleng for almost twenty-five years. He was, and is, stimulating, irritating, loyal,

* *Da Capo Press paperback, 1975.*
† *Joe Adamson, Tex Avery.*

cynical, wise, funny, stubborn, pragmatic, explosive, intelligent, impatient with stupidity, generous with everything he could think of to improve another director's pictures . . . hopeful but not demanding that you would do the same for him, irritating (this time because he could detect real weakness in a storyboard with bewildering insight and never hesitated to state it), a superb draftsman though he did not know it then and does not know it now, insane, to be sure, what else?—and yet one of the sanest men I have ever known—and the funniest—and the most innocent of his own talent.

That's a hell of a lot of attributes to carry around in one freckled head. He used to have a Friz frieze of red hair around the gray matter in that baffling skull. Yosemite Sam lived there—usually caged, but so did small birds and fluttery little old ladies and frustrated cats and voracious mice, too: one of the funniest, most thoughtful and touching cartoons of all time is *Birds Anonymous*. Try also the one about the starving mouse who tried to eat cats. Try also *Sahara Hare*, *Knighty Knight*

Friz Freleng's brilliant layout of Bugs Bunny and Yosemite Sam: BUGS BUNNY RIDES AGAIN *(1948)*

Like everyone else, our subject smoked, until 1938

Production manager Johnny Burton and Friz Freleng with Friz's Oscar

Bugs, and many others, including the two about a pair of Cockney dogs—"Spike's my hero" was the key line, just as "Friz's my hero" is mine.

Friz timed his pictures on musical bar sheets in the most beautiful tiny lettering style you ever saw. These were then transferred onto exposure sheets.

No one except Tex Avery had as perfect a sense of timing as did Friz Freleng, and no one could pre-time a picture with as absolute certainty as he could.

Live-action directors find it difficult to believe what directors at Warner Bros. cartoon division were called upon to do: pre-time and pre-edit a picture to within eight frames (one-third of a second) of its ultimate length *before* going to the camera or the animator. That's what we had to do, and the master of this arcane art was Friz Freleng.

He understood also the drollity (drollness? drolliciousness?) of failure and imperfect behavior. If Sylvester built a ladder in search of avian tiffin, he always dropped something or bent a nail or stubbed his toe, and by so doing achieved the credibility, the believability common to all great comedians. It is the sheer awkwardness of their efforts to achieve their goals that makes us relate to them, sympathize with them, and ultimately laugh with them.

Laugh *with* them—not at them. This great rule is as true of Friz Freleng's characters as it is true of Langdon, Keaton (Buster *and* Diane), and, of course, Chaplin, as well as the Chaplin of the latter-day saints, Woody Allen.

Animation as Friz Freleng directs it demonstrates the peculiar and little-understood anatomy of motion pictures in general. Many people working in the field of animation think of themselves as graphic artists, which is like a motion-picture photographer mistakenly comparing himself to a still photographer. Actually, shooting motion pictures, including animation,

and performing music are very similar indeed—one, impinging a successive series of varied sounds on the ear; the other, impinging a successive series of varied sights on the eyes. It is no coincidence then, it is just plain good sense, that Friz Freleng set down the timing of his films on musical bar sheets.

Friz is a musician as well as an excellent draftsman, and it is not surprising that many of his films are a disarming and intricate web of music (a flurry of sounds) and animation (a flurry of drawings). No student of animation can safely ignore the wizardry of these cartoons—if he can stop laughing long enough to seriously study their beauty.

To live twenty-five years with a man who could direct such pictures was not easy, because at first I hadn't the remotest idea how he did those great musicals. I know now; all you have to be is Friz Freleng.

A sampler of my favorite Freleng musical films in no particular order, but just as my fancy loves to dwell on them: RHAPSODY IN RIVETS, HOLIDAY FOR SHOESTRINGS, LIGHTS FANTASTIC, PIGS IN A POLKA, RHAPSODY RABBIT, MOUSE MAZURKA.

NOTE: If you've missed any of these Friz-directed films, you've lived a barren life:

THE FIGHTING 69TH ½, 1941; THE WABBIT WHO CAME TO SUPPER, 1942; LITTLE RED RIDING RABBIT, 1944; HOLIDAY FOR SHOE-STRINGS, 1946; A HARE GROWS IN MANHATTAN, 1947; BUCCANEER BUNNY, 1948; HIGH DIVING HARE, 1949; MOUSE MAZURKA, 1949; HIS BITTER HALF, 1950; TWEETY'S S.O.S., 1951; BIRD IN A GUILTY CAGE, 1952; A STREET CAT NAMED SYLVESTER, 1953; DR. JER-KYL'S HIDE, 1954; SAHARA HARE, 1955; HEIR CONDITIONED, 1955; TUGBOAT GRANNY, 1956; TWO CROWS FROM TACOS, 1956; TRICK OR TWEET, 1959; GOLDIMOUSE AND THE THREE CATS, 1960; REBEL WITHOUT CLAWS, 1961; THE LAST HUNGRY CAT, 1961; D'FIGHTIN' ONES, 1961; MEXICAN CAT DANCE, 1963.

Sylvester and famished mouse—layout by Friz (by the way, the technical name for a wildcat is Felis sylvestris)

THE WRITERS: THE SLUM KID, THE SCION, AND ME

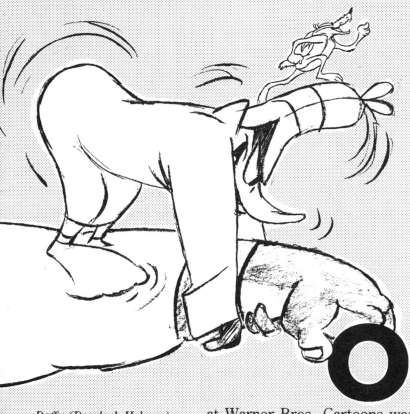

Daffy (Doorlock Holmes)
Duck and the Shropshire
Slasher: DEDUCE, YOU SAY
(1956)

Porky Pig as Dr. Watkins

One of the oddities of the writers at Warner Bros. Cartoons was that they did not write; they translated their ideas through drawings known in the trade as story sketches. Thus, our stories were in visual form from the outset. This method drives most live-action writers into creative convulsions. First of all, they cannot draw— our writers seldom drew well, but they drew well enough— and second of all: how can anyone write without all those delicious adjectives, adverbs, and rich, beautiful prose? The only words allowed on story sketches are those relating to camera moves, to dialogue, or to ensuing movement.

A six-minute cartoon usually required about 150 story sketches assembled on a storyboard 8 × 4 feet. The writer and director working together as a writing team would turn out a story for a six-minute cartoon in five weeks.

The Writers

The great directors at Warner Bros./Schlesinger were hired because they had superb reputations elsewhere: Friz Freleng at Disney and Harman-Ising; Tex Avery at Walt Lantz/Universal; Frank Tashlin from Terrytoons—and these directors demanded great writers, under the threat that they would hold their breaths and turn blue unless they had their way. It seems obvious to me that all great artists possess two essential qualities: one, their individual artistry; and two, their demand to be surrounded by talent. So the directors usually got their way, the studio was soon awash with writers such as Warren Foster, Michael Maltese, Tedd Pierce, Rich Hogan, Bob Givens, David Monahan, and many others, but occasionally Leon Schlesinger in his effort to achieve failure in the face of success would slip one through without reference to his directors. Such an acquisition was the wonderful Alex Masianof, who did everything in the world well but write. He was charming, delightful, ebullient, and enthusiastic to the point of idiocy. "I have eet, I have eet!" Alex would cry, playing the part of both Curies on the discovery of radium. "So fonny!"—he gripped his stomach in a paroxysm of delight and gasped, choked, then snapped to heel-clicking attention; he had been a Russian cavalry officer before World War I:

Pepé Le Pew responding to an Alex Masianof lyric

> The poosey ring the bell,
>   up jomped the little doggie,
> Vhere is Mister Hen?
>   She's out with the raccoon.

Bob McKimson: one of the greatest of the Warner Bros. animators

All those gathered looked dumbfounded. Alex took this for awe.

"You see how fonny? How thees kitty poosey ring the bell ho-ho in soch a fonny way? I tell you thees my frands weel be the fooniest of all theengs . . . Just you make the animation very fonny and everyone, everywhere, everythere weel laugh. Now you make fonny doggie, make fonny Mister Hen, and make very fonny the raccoon."

Turning on a benign heel, he left the room, creatively satisfied. That is the kind of cartoons we would have produced if writers were left to Leon Schlesinger's judgment.

Fortunately, the curious chemistry that brought such directors as Tex, Friz, Bob Clampett, and Frank Tashlin together also accumulated under their and my auspices three of the finest gag men/sketch artists/writers to ever grace this or any other studio: Mike Maltese, Tedd Pierce, and Warren Foster. Warren worked with Clampett, with Bob McKimson (who later became a director), and for most of his career with Friz Freleng. Tedd Pierce worked with Frank Tashlin, with me, and with Bob McKimson. Most of my life as a director I was fortunate enough to work with only two writers—the talented and funny Tedd Pierce and Michael Maltese.

Where do writers for animated cartoons come from? Very unlikely backgrounds.

Coyote realizing tardily the undependability of Acme products

*Ted Pierce, sans mustache
. . . and extra "d" added
later*

TEDD PIERCE
(Edward Stacey Pierce III)

In the heterogeneous patchwork world of the animated cartoon Edward Stacey Pierce the Third was the only scion.

SCION: [*Webster's*] A descendant or heir; a detached shoot or twig.

If the Warner Bros. cartoon unit had been the Victorian Army of India, Edward Stacey Pierce the Third would have been our "Gentleman Ranker," lamented by Kipling.

However, one would never have found Edward Stacey Pierce the Third weeping on his table down at Mory's, no "Baa, baa, baa" would ever sully the precise regimental mustache that lolled elegantly beneath the splendor of the arched beauty of his slender eagle-beak.

Edward Stacey Pierce the Third looked like C. Aubrey Smith at twenty-two playing the role of the world's foremost authority on the dry martini.

Never has a charming pixilated mind lurked beneath a more incongruous façade, because Edward Stacey Pierce the Third was a wonderful cartoon writer, gagman, story-sketch artist. He was Mickey Rooney in Ronald Colman's body. He was, in fact, Edward Stacey Pierce the Third only in his mother's hawk eyes. To us, to our everlasting delight, he was Tedd Pierce. Tedd with two "d"s. He said the extra "d" was a matter of balance in a world which he contended listed to the starboard ever since Bil Baird, the puppeteer, dropped the "l" out of Bill. Tedd felt that the world rode its axis in a more relaxed manner since he had added the "d" to Ted.

For some reason, Tedd always insisted that Bil Baird had dropped the penultimate "l" rather than the final one. "The thing would have capsized if he'd taken out the final 'l,' " he

contended. "The next-to-the-last letter in any name has had no experiencc in holding a nomenclature together, but pulling— or rather, extracting—the next-to-the-last 'l' was no danger to Baird.

"Adding a 'd' to my name," he went on, "was simply shoring up a good thing, a little insurance against a time when one of my descendants might acquire Baird's syndrome and pull a 'd.' Well, there we'd be back at the same old stand. Few people," he would say to his martini olive, "are as kind to their family tree as am I."

Tedd worked with me for several years, through an assortment of girls, wives, and assignations. His attitude toward sex was direct and uncompromising.

"When concupiscence descends upon the Road Runner," he said, "he selects a small delectable lizard and presents it to the lady of his choice. If she accepts his suggestion of a quick shack-up undcr the nearest chaparral motel, then, and only then, does he deliver his offering—*after the act, after the fact*. The Road

Pepé Le Pew in a raffish mood in CAT'S BAH (1954)

111

Runner is wise beyond his years. None of this skittering-flamingo or hooting-swan nonsense for him. He realizes that preliminaries are debilitating, wearisome, and incongruous. Both parties to a mating usually know at the outset whether or not; the rest is just a not-so-stately pavane. The Road Runner wines and lizards his girl *afterwards*, a touching tribute to a lovely affair.

"I never," Tedd went on, "offer flowers, baubles, or bubbles before an encounter, but my love and admiration and resources have no boundaries *afterwards*. I want my love to feel loved, admired, cared for, and deeply aware of my gratitude and affection. I woo her, adore her, and bedeck her in the wonderful post-coitus period, when we are relaxed, tensionless, and confident of each other."

Tedd was as honest, decent, and thoughtful a young man as ever to emerge from a fake environment: the Stacey-Pierces of Pasadena, Bar Harbor, Choate Academy, Harvard, and Wall Street. His mother, who looked like a demented Margaret Dumont posing as the Statue of Liberty, was so outraged at her eldest son that she disowned him on his fifth birthday for refusing to eat lobster. "Stacey-Pierces eat lobster, Edward.

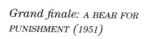

Grand finale: A BEAR FOR PUNISHMENT (1951)

Your great-grandfather ate lobster, your grandfather ate lobster, your father ate lobster, and you, Edward Stacey Pierce the Third, of that honorable line, shall eat lobster also."

The five-year-old not yet Tedd with two "d"s laughed. "It tastes like boiled daddy longlegs," he said.

If he had been stubborn, obdurate, or rebellious, she could have trotted out her many draconian skills, but like Eddie Selzer, laughter she understood not at all. That it had to do with humor she knew not at all, since humor she knew not at all. Laughter to her was as the braying of donkeys, and having ridden donkeys in Egypt, she knew by experience that her acid proclamations would have no effect on the obedience of these quadrupeds.

She could not disown a donkey, but she could disown her son. Not legally, of course, but for the rest of his life Tedd was, in her eyes, only an irritating lump on her horizon, and her entire icy affection smothered Tedd's younger brother, and her entire estate on her death ignored Tedd entirely in favor of his fawning sibling.

Perhaps Tedd's final touching relationship with his mother can best be demonstrated by this incident:

"Shortly after her death," he said, "I wandered into my brother's house in Laguna Beach and there, staring down at me from the mantelpiece, was the urn containing my mother's ashes. I uncorked the quart mayonnaise jar of martinis that I carried in case of emergency and sat down on the ottoman and thought evil thoughts about Mother. But after the jar had been emptied well below the Best Foods label, all the rough edges had worn off and my lachrimation had replaced the Margaret (Wicked Witch) Hamilton of my memories with a sort of *zaftig* white Aunt Jemima. Perhaps I had wronged the old bird, perhaps she was not a vulture but a dove? Crying softly as I drained the mayonnaise jar, I achieved a final and noble gesture, a gallantry,

Witch Hazel (voice by beautiful, brilliant June Foray)—polishing her cutlery

*Early lobby cards for
theater display*

a beau-ideal gesture for any misunderstood mother. Carrying the casket before me like the Holy Grail, I went out onto the windswept moonlit beach. With my back to the wind and my mother between my knees, I braved the breakers in our old skiff. Beyond the waves I stood up and turned, opening the urn: 'Mother, I ask your forgiveness for never understanding how understanding you really were. I consign your sacred ashes to the sea you loved so well,' and in one dramatic swoop I did consign her ashes to the brisk onshore breeze. Back came Mother's ashes to blind me, choke me, and cake my loving face. Falling backward into the scuppers, I managed to lose both oars, which—as it turned out—was just as well, since being blind, I probably would have rowed out into the ocean and drowned. As it was, I drifted around, finally going ashore a mile or so down the beach. It took three days to wash Mother completely off my face, but her opinion of me remained as clearly stated in death as it was in life."

Tedd worked with me as a writer-gag man for several years, a source of constant surprise and unanticipated delight. His disdain of artifice and fat prose served me well. He wrote with me some of the best of my early films:

THE NIGHT WATCHMAN, 1938

LITTLE LION HUNTER (*With Bob Givens; birth of the Mynah Bird*), 1939

ELMER'S CANDID CAMERA (*With Rich Hogan; embryonic Bugs and Elmer*), 1940

GHOST WANTED (*With Dave Monahan*), 1940
(*A small boy ghost several years before Casper*)

BEDTIME FOR SNIFFLES (*With Rich Hogan*), 1940

INKI AND THE LION (*With Rich Hogan*), 1941

THE DRAFT HORSE, 1942

THE SQUAWKIN' HAWK (*Introducing Henery Hawk*), 1942

THE DOVER BOYS, 1942
CASE OF THE MISSING HARE, 1942
SUPER-RABBIT, 1943
WACKIKI WABBIT, 1943
ODOR-ABLE KITTY (*First introduction of Pepé Le Pew*), 1945

Plus the following dialogue sheets from *Rocket Squad*, a take-off of the old *Dragnet* TV show.

ROCKET SQUAD 1956

Writer: Tedd Pierce PRODUCTION NO. 1347

*Daffy as a Webb-footed Joe
Monday and his partner,
Porky Tuesday*

1. DAFFY: (Narrator) This is the Milky Way . . . a nice galaxy . . . Eight hundred and seventy-five billion trillion people live here . . . Yes, it's a nice place to live . . . It's my job to keep it that way . . . I'm a space cop. My name's Monday. My partner's name is Tuesday. He always follows me. It was Wednesday, January 23, 10:26 p.m.

2. PORKY: T-ten twenty-*eight*!

3. DAFFY: It was 10:28 p.m. . . . We were returning from a routine investigation in the Big Dipper area . . . a 712 . . . Malicious mischief . . . Schoolchildren had blown the ring off Saturn . . . When will parents learn to keep uranium out of their children's reach?

4. PORKY: Yeh . . . wh-when?

5. DAFFY: 10:34 . . . Headquarters called.

6. CAPTAIN: Calling Prowl Jet 36 . . . Prowl Jet 36 . . . Come in, 36 . . . Over.

7. DAFFY: Joe Monday.

8. PORKY: O-over.
9. CAPTAIN: Joe . . . It's the Flying Saucer Bandit again . . . First National Bank of Jupiter! Report in!
10. DAFFY: Wilco!
11. DAFFY: Wednesday, January 23 . . . 10:42 p.m.
12. PORKY: T-ten forty-*six*!
13. DAFFY: 10:46 p.m. . . . We returned to Headquarters.
14. PORKY: Isn't modern science wonderful? People used to have to use stairs!
15. DAFFY: 10:52 . . . Back at the old desk . . . waiting for a call from the Chief . . . Half a cop's life is spent in waiting . . . 10:53 . . . The Chief called.
16. CAPTAIN: Joe . . . come right over, please! I need your help immediately!
17. DAFFY: Right!
18. DAFFY: My interview with the Chief was brief and to the point . . . He wanted me to find out who the Flying Saucer Bandit was and then to place him under arrest.

19. DAFFY: I consented.
20. CHIEF: (Kisses Daffy's feet)
21. DAFFY: 11:07 . . . We proceeded to the scene of the crime.
22. DAFFY: 11:21 . . . Checked in at scene of crime.
23. DAFFY: The crime robots were on the job.
24. DAFFY: They were searching out and collecting vital bits of evidence . . . picking up suspicious footprints . . . gathering up all significant objects. No clue is too small to escape their notice.

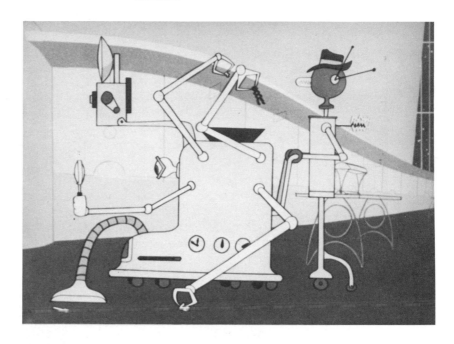

25. DAFFY: 12:15 a.m. . . . We returned to Headquarters with the clues.
25a. PORKY: A c-cop's life isn't all beer and skittles.
26. DAFFY: Now all the facilities of a great modern crime lab were brought to bear.

27.	DAFFY:	We identified the name of that song.
28.	DAFFY:	"Mother Machree."
29.	DAFFY:	We proceeded to the Machree file . . .
30.	DAFFY:	It was a long one . . .
31.	DAFFY:	We finally found what we were after . . .
32.	DAFFY:	This criminal was so clever he'd never been suspected of anything.
33.	DAFFY:	The case was beginning to heat up. Our next step was the crimino-detecto set.

High-tech crime detection board

34.	DAFFY:	Machree was found to be at Elsa's Blast-In . . . selecting a sandwich.
35.	DAFFY:	12:40 a.m. He selected a pastrami on rye with mustard. That figured.
36.	DAFFY:	We didn't have much time . . . He was a notorious fast eater.
37.	DAFFY:	1:07 . . . He left the Blast-In.
38.	DAFFY:	1:08 . . . We arrived at the Blast-In . . . Our deductions later proved that we had missed him by one minute.
39.	DAFFY:	1:09 . . . We set out in pursuit.

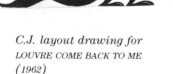

I DIN'T DO NOTHIN !!
I..DIN'T DO NOTHIN'!

The "Flying Saucer Bandit"
with an unlikely alibi:
ROCKET SQUAD *(1956)*

40. DAFFY: If cops won't obey traffic regulations . . . how can we expect others to?

41. PORKY: 10:23 . . . We lost him in a large smog bank over Los Angeles.

42. PORKY: Hey . . . J-Joe . . . get a load of this.

43. DAFFY: (Loudspeaker) All right, Machree . . . we know you're in there! Come on out!

44. DAFFY: Like all criminals, he had an elaborate alibi prepared.

45. MACHREE: I didn't do nothin' . . . I didn't do nothin'! Like I said, I didn't do nothin'!

46. NARRATOR: This case was brought to trial April 23, 10:00 a.m. in Ultra Superior Court 13527B, Department of Astral Justice . . . As a result of this trial . . . the two arresting officers were sentenced to twenty years for false arrest . . .

47. PORKY: Th-thirty years . . .

C.J. layout drawing for
LOUVRE COME BACK TO ME
(1962)

It was only logical, of course, that Tedd would be in on the beginnings of Pepé Le Pew. If ever there was another pogo stick, it was Tedd Pierce. His devotion to women was at times pathetic, at times psychological, but always enthusiastic. Just as Pepé Le Pew could not envisage that any female would run away from him ("She is seeking for herself a trysting place. Alors, for the trysting place I can wait"), so Tedd could not really believe that any woman could honestly refuse his honestly stated need for her. He was Beau Ideal, Beau Sabreur, and Beau Geste all at once, with accent on the Geste. (It would have been impossible to have worked with Tedd and *not* come up with the idea of Pepé Le Pew.)

119

MICHAEL MALTESE

Michael Maltese, as he put it, was born of poor but Italian parents on a tiny island in the Atlantic—Manhattan.

Actually, Mike was born on the Lower East Side of Manhattan when "lower" meant just that: low. His mother, I believe, was the proprietor of a tiny candy store below the street level of the five-story tenement where Mike was born and where his family lived.

He remembered being designated as a "slum child" by slumming ladies from the Upper West Side, which in 1916 was the most elegant section, facing Central Park.

"Mabel, look at the poor little slum child!" they probably

exclaimed, delighted naturalists identifying a new species of toad. The slum child was not offended, because he had never heard the word "child" before, much less "slum."

"How many bathrooms are there in this building?"—pencil poised over notebook, inquired the tall lady of the small, bright-eyed slum child.

"Bathroom? What's witha the bathroom?" The slum child was genuinely puzzled.

"Oh yes, of course, ahh, toilets—how many toilets?" Just what value such knowledge would have was not clear to anyone, including the lady who asked.

"Toy-let?" The slum child mulls over this new word. "Toy-let? Oh! Yeah. You mean crap room. All of us has one."

Still blushing, but delighted, too—this is the real stuff!—our female Henry Ward Beecher persisted: "Each family has its own toilet?"

The slum child was astonished. "Nah—what's each fambly?—one crap room per each floor, whattaya think?"

Horrified: "You mean, each toilet must serve the residents of an entire floor!?"

"Look, lady"—the slum child was being extremely patient—"there's only twenty-fi, thirty people on each floor, everybody craps on a average maybe once, twice a day. Takes you maybe ten, twelve minutes a time each crap, don't it? Peein's much faster—one, two minutes—plenty a time for everbody—whattaya have in mind, one crap room for each 'n every fambly in a house?" Laughs. "Hey, Florio, lady here thinks every poison in New York should have his very ownliest private crap room!"

The pushcart peddlers, the fat ladies leaning on second-floor pillows get into the hilarious act, whole-Italian-hearted laughter at the wonderful idea of a one person, one crap room. Amid this undignified cacophony, the fashionable ladies unfashionably retreat.

1950: Sixteen animators and two Oscars: FOR SCENT-IMENTAL REASONS (best animated cartoon) and SO MUCH FOR SO LITTLE (best documentary short subject)—left to right, back row: Phil De Guard, Lloyd Vaughan, Madilyn Wood, Paul Julian, Roy Laufenburger, Abe Levitow, Dapper Director, Bob Gribbroek, Mike Maltese, Keith Darling, Marilyn Wood (bearing startling resemblance to her twin sister, Madilyn, q.v.), Ken Harris, Ben Washam; front row: Pete Alvarado, Richard Thompson, Phil Monroe

ONE FROGGY EVENING (1955):
Construction worker as
Michigan J. Frog emerges
from cornerstone

Worker sees financial
advantage in singing
frog . . .

and kidnaps him, thereby
guaranteeing a life of
frustration: singing frogs
will sing only for their
owners

Mike grew into his teens to become a plumber's helper—installing basic pipes and conduits, reaming metallic intestines together to form the necessary iron alimentary canals to make livable the skeletal frames of newborn apartment buildings. An honorable but often dangerous trade, particularly so in the winter, when frozen winds and icy iron make the plumber's slippery high-steel act dangerously precarious. Mike said the danger didn't concern him but the cold did, which was brought into focus one fateful frosty January morning with the Arctic wind keening through the snowy girders when he opened the door to the wooden shack where his overalls were stored. They were, he said, frozen stiff, literally—frozen stiff in a sort of jumping, knee-bent position, just as he had removed them the preceding night.

"I immediately decided, then and there," he later told me, "that whatever the future might hold for me, I would never again work at any job that required, as a condition of employment, that I wear frozen overalls."

Without qualm, or a second thought, or worry about an uncertain future, he slid and skittered down fourteen flights and out onto Broadway. Letting pure chance lead his feet, he turned east on 40-somethingth Street, checking each window, ashcan, doorway for a key to his expectations, with no harbinger, no bluebird of gladness, to guide him. Then destiny planted a small sign in the window of a rather tallish, ramshackle, run-down building: "In-betweeners Wanted. Apply 18th Floor."

"I didn't know," Mike told me, "an in-betweener from a go-between. Riding up in a rickety, wobbly elevator, I found the name *Terrytoons* on an eighteenth-floor glass door. Somehow I knew that I was home. I had always had the knack of making terrible drawings that seemed funny, and funny was precisely what the Terrytoons studio was looking for. At the ensuing interview with Paul Terry I suggested a slogan for his spastic

122

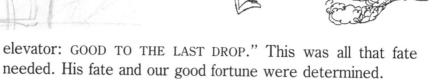

elevator: GOOD TO THE LAST DROP." This was all that fate needed. His fate and our good fortune were determined.

After a year or so at Terrytoons, and by devious routes (he could not drive a car), Mike emigrated to Warners in the late 1930s and eventually became my associate, my friend, my gag man, and writer extraordinary for most of the days of my life as a director.

The quirky brilliance of his ready wit was never neutral. He disdained facts as useless—only the odd, the unusual, the hilariously peculiar interested him.

All things, all people were, in Mike's mind, related to each other in some undiscovered ways. The fun lay in the marriage of oddities: a French skunk in a perfume shop; a male rabbit singing Brünnhilde's role against a mighty eighty-piece symphony orchestra; a singing frog driving a simple man into a diabolical frustration. With people his attitude and philosophy remained constant; their personalities most interested him when most skewed.

One hundred years later, a "building disintegrator" worker finds the frog in another cornerstone . . .

and sees financial advantages . . .

and kidnaps frog . . . iris out

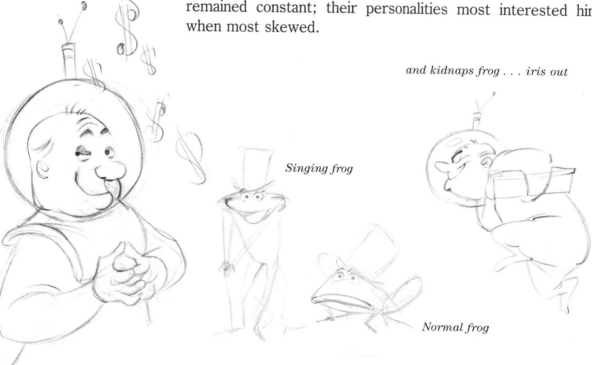

Singing frog

Normal frog

At the studio Mike struck up a friendly friendship with a girl named Henrietta Hultz. She interested him, I think, because she didn't appear to be either a girl or a boy. She was thin as only bamboo is thin, and her hair hung in a gray mass, like secondhand noodles.

One day Mike and I were walking down the hall and came upon a wet, bedraggled gray mop splayed flat on the floor.

Mike struck his forehead. "My God, Henrietta's fainted."

However, the case of the extension cord brought me into absolute harmony with Mike. When creative ineptitude meets creative ineptitude, bonds far stronger than steel are formed.

Mike's problem was to get an extension cord from outlet A over the door to position B. His early Elmo Lincoln circa frame house having few electrical outlets.

A twenty-five-foot extension cord was quickly purchased, along with a half pound of brads. It was the work of but an hour or two to run the wire up and over the doorway, secure this wire with brads every few inches or so—an effective if not artistic job accomplished.

But how to anchor the outlet to the wall? It did not occur to Mike, nor would it have occurred to me, to unscrew the plate as instructed and firmly anchor the plate to the wall with a single screw or nail.

Mike's work was far more picturesque, and effective, too, in its poetic way. He simply pounded nails all the way around the plate and bent them over to hold the plate: the result looking like nothing so much as a multilegged metallic spider embedded in the plaster.

Although logic and believability are the essence of humor, we never had to question or ask for logic from one another. No explanation was ever necessary. "It works or it doesn't work, it's that simple." Our units did not compete with each other or with others within the studio or, indeed, in other

Michael Maltese
by Michael Maltese

studios; artistry is only a footrace against yourself. Just so, Mike and I followed only the imps of our own perverse creativity, confident of the unexpected, inhibited only by inevitable occasional puddles of the commonplace. Just as the squirrel cannot explain or even be aware of his symbiotic relationship with the redwood, Mike and I never knew which of us was the squirrel and which the redwood.

Just a few of the films I was lucky enough to work on with Mike Maltese:

MOUSE WRECKERS (*Hubie and Bertie*), 1949
FAST AND FURRY-OUS (*First Coyote and Road Runner*), 1949
FRIGID HARE, 1949

and

FOR SCENT-IMENTAL REASONS   1949

(Academy Award Winner)

Writer: Mike Maltese   PRODUCTION NO. 1104

PROPRIETOR: (Sings)
               La shave wa zay de mwa . . .
               De mwa la shave wa zay . . .
               Wee Wee la toot la la . . .
               Lay voo lay voovoo . . .

               Toot sweet oon toot sweet toot . . .
               On shay voo zem my foot . . .
               Oh vouto rooney zoot . . .
               Ze coo-coo . . .
               (Hums to self)

PROPRIETOR: *Sacray maroon!!*

PROPRIETOR: *Assistancion!! Assistancion!!! Gendarme!! Poilu!! Le help!!* (Into distance)

PROPRIETOR: *Le help! Aide! Assistancion!! Gendarme!!*

PROPRIETOR: *Aide! Assistancion!! Mon pauvre parfumes!! Gendarme!!* (Hysterical)

PROPRIETOR: *Avec!! Aide!! Mon petite establishment!!! Ruination!! Catastrophe!!* (Pants)

GENDARME: Pouf, Joseph! Gendarme kel lay feex!

PROPRIETOR: Por thonk . . . gallant Gendarme . . . merci beaucoup le thonks . . .

GENDARME: *Sacray cerise!!! Le Pew!!!!*

SKUNK: (Sings) Affair d'amour . . . Affair d'coeur . . . Je ne say quois . . . je vis en espoir . . . (Sniffs) Mmmm m mm . . . un smella voo feenay . . . (Hums)

GENDARME: *Le kittee kel terriblay odeur!!*

GENDARME: Pard'm wa . . . Jo-seph . . . apray midi le fudge is burning!!

PROPRIETOR: *Allay Gendarme!! Allay!! Return'mwa!! This instonce!!* Oh, pauvre mwa, I am ze bankrupt . . . (Sobs)

CAT: Le mew . . . Le purrrrrrrr.

PROPRIETOR: *A-a-ahhh.* Le pussee ferocious! Remove zot skunk! Zot cat-pole from ze premises!! *Avec!!*

CAT: (Smells skunk) Sniff, sniff, sniff-sniff, sniff-sniff.

SKUNK: Quel es? . . . Ahhh . . . la belle femme skunk fatale!! tch-tch.

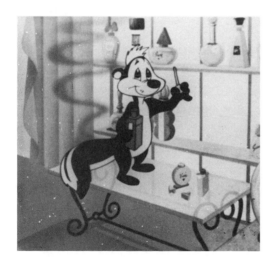

SKUNK: Ahh . . . my little dar-ling . . . eet is lov' at first sight, is it not? No? (Kiss, kiss, kiss) Do not come wiz me to ze Casbah . . . We shall makes beyootiful musics togezzer *right here!* Ah, ze l'amour!! Aaah, ze toujours!! Ahhh, ze l'amour!!! (Kiss kiss kiss kiss kiss)

SKUNK: Honh?

SKUNK:	Ah . . . the small one . . . she is make herself dainty for me . . . for ze daintiness I can wait . . . Alouette . . . shentee alouette . . . alouette . . . the time is up, dainty or not, we continue wiz ze wooing . . .
SKUNK:	Zis little love bundle . . . now she is seeking for us . . . a trysting place . . . Touching . . . is it not?
SKUNK:	Come, my little peanut of brittle . . . I will help you . . . wait for me . . . *Wait!* I am the corn-beef to you, ze cab-baj . . .
SKUNK:	Where are you . . . cab-baj?
SKUNK:	Nom de plume! What ees thees? Ze cab-baj do not run away from ze corn-beef!! But wait! (Small) But ah-ah . . . now it is clear zis clevaire rabbit want to play hid-go and I seek her . . .
SKUNK:	Lookout, pigeon . . . I am going to see you . . . *Ah!!* There you are!! I am coming to see you!!
SKUNK:	*Ah ze amour!! Ahhh ze abandon!!! Ohhh ze madness!!!*
COO-COO:	We're not easily upset in Grand Rapids . . . geek . . . goot, glk . . . but how Grand Rapids can you get? (Into whips again)
SKUNK:	Where are you, pigeon . . . ? I am looking for you . . . I am going . . . huh?
SKUNK:	I meesed . . . fortunately for you!! So now, mon cherie, we can begins life anew . . . mmmm (Kiss kiss kiss kiss)
SKUNK:	C'est la guerre. (Philosophically)
SKUNK:	'Allo, bby . . .
SKUNK:	I am ze lock-smith of love, no?
SKUNK:	Com dar-ling, we most be grown-up about zis

"Lookout, pigeon"

128

theeng . . . do not run away from ze love . . .
Here? What is thees? (Small) Oh . . . but of
course, thees little one weesh to commit suicide
to prove her love for me . . . what a sweet
gesture . . . nevertheless, I must prevent
it . . .

SKUNK: *Saved!!*

SKUNK: Viva l'amour! We die togezzer!!

SKUNK: I am not dead . . . no?

CAT: (Muffled) *Ahhh . . . choo!* Sniff, sniffle. (Cold
sounds)

SKUNK: What's thees? Is that you, pigeon? Is that . . .
hanh? Oh . . . pardon . . . Grand-ma-ma . . .
but have you seen a beeyootiful young lady
skunk . . .

CAT: (Cold sounds: sneezes, sniffles, little sneezes.
More sniffles)

SKUNK: Where are you, pigeon? . . . hmmmmm . . . I
am looking somewhere to find you . . . Yoo-hoo
rabbit, where are you, humm?

CAT: (More cold sounds . . . separate sneezes and
sniffles and inhales)

SKUNK: Ah-ha . . . Perhaps you have return in here . . . Are you here, then . . . golden girl? Eh . . . who is thees? . . . Oh, it is you again, my ancient . . . what can I do . . . to . . . help . . . you . . . heh . . . why do you lock ze . . . (Small) Oh no . . .

SKUNK: Control yourself, madame . . . you cannot be in earnest . . . ha-ha . . . a joke . . . yes? Ha-ha . . . no.

SKUNK: You know, it is possible to be *too* attractive!

and

BEAR FEAT, 1949
THE RABBIT OF SEVILLE, 1950

and

RABBIT FIRE   1951

Writer: Mike Maltese   PRODUCTION NO. 1166

1. ELMER: (Tiptoeing through the forest) Shhhhhh! Be vewy, vewy quiet . . . I'm hunting wabbits, heh-heh-heh.
2. ELMER: *Oh boy!! Wabbit twacks!!*
3. DAFFY: Oh, Buggsy . . . Buggsy pal! There's a friend here to see you!!
4. DAFFY: Thurvival of the fittest! . . . and besides . . . it's fun!!
5. BUGS: Did someone knock?
6. BUGS: (Slightly perturbed) Eh . . . what's up, Doc?
7. ELMER: Now I got you . . . you wabbit!! Heh-heh-heh . . .

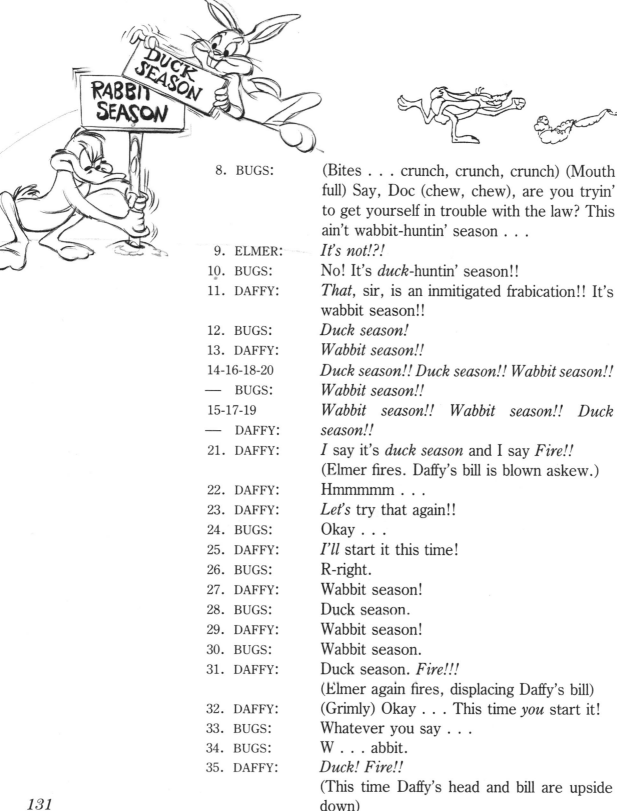

8. BUGS: (Bites . . . crunch, crunch, crunch) (Mouth full) Say, Doc (chew, chew), are you tryin' to get yourself in trouble with the law? This ain't wabbit-huntin' season . . .

9. ELMER: *It's not!?!*

10. BUGS: No! It's *duck*-huntin' season!!

11. DAFFY: *That*, sir, is an inmitigated frabication!! It's wabbit season!!

12. BUGS: *Duck season!*

13. DAFFY: *Wabbit season!!*

14-16-18-20 *Duck season!! Duck season!! Wabbit season!!*
— BUGS: *Wabbit season!!*

15-17-19 *Wabbit season!! Wabbit season!! Duck*
— DAFFY: *season!!*

21. DAFFY: *I* say it's *duck season* and I say *Fire!!*
(Elmer fires. Daffy's bill is blown askew.)

22. DAFFY: Hmmmmm . . .

23. DAFFY: *Let's* try that again!!

24. BUGS: Okay . . .

25. DAFFY: *I'll* start it this time!

26. BUGS: R-right.

27. DAFFY: Wabbit season!

28. BUGS: Duck season.

29. DAFFY: Wabbit season!

30. BUGS: Wabbit season.

31. DAFFY: Duck season. *Fire!!!*
(Elmer again fires, displacing Daffy's bill)

32. DAFFY: (Grimly) Okay . . . This time *you* start it!

33. BUGS: Whatever you say . . .

34. BUGS: W . . . abbit.

35. DAFFY: *Duck! Fire!!*
(This time Daffy's head and bill are upside down)

131

36.	DAFFY:	Whatha matter . . . Everythingth upside down . . .
37.	DAFFY:	Can't make headth or tailth of thingth . . .
38.	ELMER:	*Hey, you!! Come back here!!!* (Tries gun, only a click)
39.	ELMER:	Well, whaddaya know . . . no more buwwets!
40.	BUGS:	(Affected surprise) No more buwwets? (Turns to Daffy) Hey, laughing boy, no more buwwets!
41.	DAFFY:	No more *buwwets*?
42.	DAFFY:	Here!! Lemme *see* that thing!! (Snatches gun on "see")
43.	DAFFY:	Hmmmmm . . .

44.	ELMER:	(Delighted) Well, what do ya know . . . *one* buwwet left!!
45.	BUGS:	(Delighted, too) *One* buwwet weft? (Turns to Daffy) Hey, laughing boy, there was . . .
46.	DAFFY:	I know! *I know!!!*
47.	DAFFY:	(Reads sign "Duck Season") Hummmm . . .

(Turns to audience) Devilishly clever . . . (Hears Elmer coming. Quickly dresses like a rabbit) Oh oh . . .

48. DAFFY: (Imitating Bugs) Eh . . . what's up, Doc? (Bite, chew, chew) Having any luck with those ducks . . . it's duck season, y'know . . .

49. BUGS: (Dressed as and imitating Daffy) *Just* a darn minute . . . where d'ya get that *duck*-season stuff?

50. DAFFY: (Still as Bugs) Says so . . . right over on that sign (sign has changed to "Rabbit Season" again), you're so smart.

51. DAFFY: You know what to do with that gun, Doc!

52. DAFFY: (Himself now; with controlled hatred) You're dethpicable!

53. DAFFY: (Getting a little out of control; at a loss for words) Yes, you're dethpicable . . . and . . . and . . . picable . . . and . . . and . . . very definitely dethpicable . . . How a person can get *so* dethpicable in *one* lifetime is beyond me . . . It isn't as though I haven't met a lot of people . . . Goodneth knows it isn't *that*!! It's not that goodneth knows . . . (Reaction to Bugs) It ithn't . . . it . . .

54. BUGS: (Pulls cookbook out of hole and reads) Spitted duck Florentine with horseradish . . . nice . . . Filet of duck Bordelaise, maître d' butter . . . yum-yum . . .

55. BUGS: Duck Polonaise under glass . . . *mm* . . . mmmmmmmm.

56. DAFFY: (Daffy grabs book of his own) Rabbit au gratin de gelatine under tooled leather . . . drool, drool . . .

57. BUGS: Barbecued duck meat with broiled duck bill milanese . . . Yum-my yum!!

58. DAFFY: Chicken fried rabbit with cotton-tail sauce braised in carrots . . . umh, mmmmmm . . .

59. ELMER: I'm sorry, fewwas, but I'm a vegetarian . . . I just hunt for the sport of it!!! Heh-heh-heh . . .

60. BUGS: *Oh yeah?* Well, there's other sports besides hunting, y'know!

61. DAFFY: (Daffy leaps into scene with tennis racquet and sloppy shorts) *Anyone for tennis!!?* (Elmer fires. Daffy's beak slips sideways)

62. DAFFY: (Goofy) Niceth game!!

63. ELMER: Now, you scwewy wabbit . . . You're next!! (Daffy and Bugs run, dive into hole)

64. BUGS: (Hoarse whisper) Take a peek and see if he's still around.

65. DAFFY: Okay . . . (Daffy pulls self up. Offstage a gun fires)

66. BUGS: Still there?

67. DAFFY: (Slightly goofy) Still lurking about . . .

68. BUGS: I tell you what . . . you go up and make like a decoy and lure him away . . .

69. DAFFY: (Goofy) No more for me, thankth . . . I'm drivin'.

70. BUGS: Ah . . . well . . . like they say . . . never send a duck to do a rabbit's job . . .

71.	ELMER:	All wight . . . Come out or I'll bwast you out!!!
72.	BUGS:	Hmmmmm.
73.	BUGS:	(Bugs up out of hole) For *shame*, Doc!! Huntin' rabbits with an elephant gun!
74.	ELMER:	*Ewephant gun?*
75.	BUGS:	That's right, Doc . . . So why don't ya go shoot yerself an elephant? (Elephant walks in on hind legs)
76.	ELEPHANT:	(A la Joe Besser) *You do . . . and I'll give you such a pinch!!*

| 77. | ELMER: | (Furious) Just wait'll I get that scwewy wabbit and that scwewball duck . . . I'll wip'm to bits . . . I'll bwast 'em . . . O.o.o.h . . . I know they're awound here somepwace . . . I can pwactically smew them!! |

78.	DAFFY:	(On four legs like dog) Sniff . . . sniff . . . *brow . . . row . . . rowfff* . . . Sniff . . . sniff . . . sniff . . . *Brow row row!!* (Hesitates, points) Rrrrrr-r-r-r . . .
79.	ELMER:	Hey!! What's the big idea!!?? Why dontcha look where . . . *huh*!
80.	BUGS:	(Dressed as girl hunter) Oh!! How simply dreadful!!
81.	BUGS:	(Same) You poor little man . . . Did I hurt you with my naughty gun!!??
82.	DAFFY:	(Sniffs around Elmer's feet)
83.	ELMER:	(Embarrassed) Shucks . . . well . . . I . . . Ha-ha-ha . . .
84.	BUGS:	(Kisses Elmer lightly on cheek) There! Now it feels better, doesn't it?
85.	DAFFY:	(Growls) Arrrrgh . . . (Bites Elmer)
86.	ELMER:	*Yeowwww!!*
87.	DAFFY:	(Pants like dog)

88.	BUGS:	(Still as girl) Gypsy! You naughty bow-wow . . . Stop that!!
89.	ELMER:	(Furious) *O.K., wabbit . . . I see through that disguise!! Say your pwayers!!*
90.	ELMER:	*You too . . . duck!!!* (Daffy and Bugs to tree. Start ripping off sign)
91.	DAFFY:	(Normal) Wabbit season!
92.	BUGS:	(Normal) Duck season!
93-95-97-99 —	DAFFY:	*Wabbit season!! Wabbit season!! Wabbit season!!! Wabbit season!!!*
94-96-98-100 —	BUGS:	*Duck season!! Duck season!! Duck season!! Duck season!!* (Bugs pulls off last poster. Under it is a sign "Elmer Season" with a picture of Elmer)

101.	ELMER:	(Very small) Oh oh.
102.	BUGS AND DAFFY IN UNISON:	(Dressed as hunters) Shhh . . . be vewy, vewy quiet . . . We're hunting Elmers . . . Heh . heh . heh . . .

OH BWOON*HILDA*.

And the list goes on:

FEED THE KITTY, 1952
BEEP, BEEP, 1952
RABBIT SEASONING, 1952
DON'T GIVE UP THE SHEEP, 1953
DUCK AMUCK, 1953
DUCK DODGERS IN THE 24½ CENTURY, 1953
BULLY FOR BUGS, 1953
DUCK! RABBIT! DUCK!, 1953
BEWITCHED BUNNY, 1954
FROM A TO Z-Z-Z-Z, 1954
BEANSTALK BUNNY, 1955
ONE FROGGY EVENING, 1955
ALI BABA BUNNY, 1957
ROBIN HOOD DAFFY, 1958

. . . and, of course:

WHAT'S OPERA, DOC?, 1957

Elmer as Siegfried

YOU'RE SO WOVEWY!

Director and writer about to lower the boom on Herr Wagner: WHAT'S OPERA, DOC? *(1957)*

138

Ben Washam
by Ben Washam

*Yosemite Sam letting off
steam so Friz Freleng
doesn't have to*

Our writers were not writers, our writers were gag men, story-sketch men, comedians, they did everything an animated cartoon needed, except write. So it was a surprise to me on my sixty-ninth birthday to discover that all the time there had been a real writer lurking on my staff posing as animator: Ben Washam.

Ben Washam, like nearly all the animators I knew in more than fifty years as a director in animation, came from an unlikely source. He was born in the backcountry of the Arkansas Ozarks, and in his speech, parts of that murky idiom still surfaced. His most violent expletive, when he was thoroughly upset, was: "Thunder over Possum-foot Bridge!" or, when frustrated: "Thanks for the sour persimmons, cousin." He became a truly great animator, one of the most sensitive, one of the most subtle—able to extract laughter by the quirk of a ducky eyebrow, the flick of a rabbit's eye. He was kind and gentle as well as talented beyond belief, but until just before his death I never knew he could write. On my sixty-ninth birthday he wrote the following letter, and in reading it over now, I wonder whether I can ever approach in writing anything so clear and so honest or whether any of us had greater claim to the term "writer" than Ben Washam.

Dear Chuck—

On my tenth birthday my father gave me a mule. It was truly love at first sight. I named him Spencer after a rifle I saw advertised in a Sears, Roebuck catalog.

The spring and summer that followed were the most wonderful in my memory. We rode over and through every hill and swamp in northeast Arkansas.

In the fall after the crops were in, everybody went to the county fair, especially Spencer and me.

Aside from judging cows, pigs, chickens, cakes, pies and the like, stump pulling was a community favorite.

The stumps were dynamited out of the ground (a few days before the fair started), then a mule was hitched to the stump. The mule that pulled the stump the greatest distance won—Spencer and me won.

First prize was a Rhode Island Red Rooster and a blue ribbon with Robert E. Lee's face painted on it with gold paint. I was so proud I kissed Spencer. Everybody laughed and my mother made me wash my face.

At this time I learned about evil. I learned evil lurks in unsuspected places and, like a spider, attacks without warning.

An aunt, who later turned out to be unsavory, invited me to have a soda pop with her.

Leaving Spencer eating hay and my rooster tied to a wagon wheel, we went off to the refreshment tent.

Everything was fine. I even got a piece of cake. The soda pop was great—I saved half of it for Spencer.

When I returned to the wagon, Spencer was gone. I grabbed a pitchfork and went looking for the thief. After looking all over the fairgrounds they finally told me that

some Yankee from Chicago gave my father fifty dollars for Spencer.

My devastation was completed that evening—my mother cooked my rooster for supper.

I spent the next day planning revenge. The thought of putting a water moccasin in my father's bed was pleasant. Then it occurred to me that anybody that mean wouldn't be troubled by a water moccasin. By the end of the day I had concluded that I couldn't fight them, but I could make sure that I never became one of them—so I made a vow never to become an adult, or care for an adult.

To make sure that I would never break the vow, I ate a green persimmon—eating a green persimmon was a sure way to test a person's sincerity. Anyone who would eat a green persimmon to back up their word had to be honest. That was especially true in courtships—however, I don't remember ever hearing of any girl eating a green persimmon.

From that time I walked into the hills and valleys of life, secure in the knowledge that I was free from adults, Yankees and unsavory aunts in particular. (It was my aunt who lured me away from Spencer with the promise of a soda pop. Deep in my heart I know that old harridan dwells in the north side of hell with all the Yankees.)

I have mellowed over the years. My vow has not been broken, only bent a little. So it is that I can tell you that you are one of the few adults I have come to love and respect.

My reason for telling you this is because I want to wish you a happy birthday and impress upon you that such a wish coming from me is no small effort.

Panorama shot of Porky ("Comedy Relief") Pig: DRIPALONG DAFFY (1951)

Ben

DUCK DODGERS: A CASE HISTORY— STORY THROUGH ANIMATION

Porky Pig as the "eager young space cadet": DUCK DODGERS IN THE 24½ CENTURY (1953)

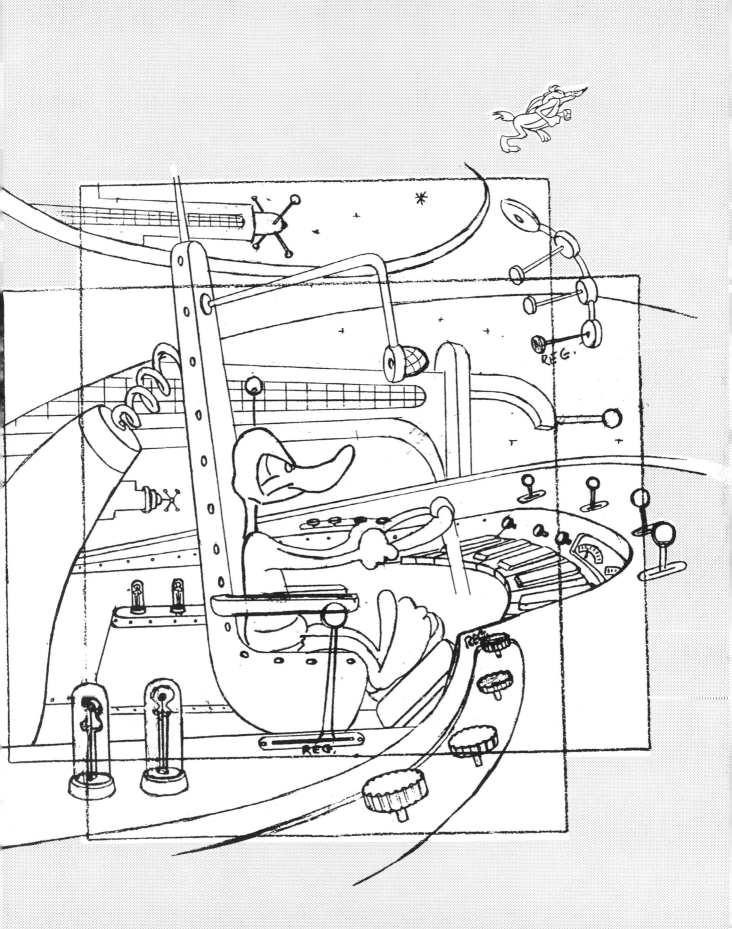

"Where did you find the motif of your divine Ninth Symphony?" Anton Bruckner was once asked. "I was on a tramp through the hills," he reportedly replied, "and climbed a crag to enjoy the view and eat my lunch. As I unfolded the greasy paper around a piece of rather strong cheese, the damned thing popped into my mind."

Re-creation of Ralph Wolf (né Wile E. Coyote) and Sam Sheepdog, clocking in to work: A SHEEP IN THE DEEP *(1962)*

All the good ideas I ever had came to me while I was milking a cow.

— GRANT WOOD

"**W**here do you get your ideas?"

This is the most common question asked by would-be animators, writers, directors.

Where do you get your ideas? Is there a rack, a file someplace where iced or quick-frozen ideas are stored, only waiting to be thawed?

I am grateful to be able to answer the question sincerely and honestly: I don't know where ideas come from.

Friz Freleng layout of Sylvester and Tweety Bird: happy symbiotic relationship between cat and bird

In looking back on a lifetime of writing, drawing, and directing stories and discovering ideas, I can see that ideas *do* seem to have a few distinctive features in common. All ideas for me seem to be based on variations of observable human behavior. Bugs Bunny is simply, and only, trying to remain alive in a world of predators; Elmer Fudd does not consider himself a predator, but a simple sportsman—he only hunts for the "thwill" of it; Daffy Duck is simply trying to get ahead; Porky in his adult life is simply a bemused spectator of the human scene; Pepé Le Pew is simply trying to get a girl; Friz Freleng's Yosemite Sam is simply trying to control his disastrous temper; Wile E. Coyote and Sylvester are simply trying to get something to eat. The trouble is that each of them has become addicted to only one form of nutriment: Friz's Tweety Bird is champagne to Sylvester; the Road Runner is caviar to the Coyote. Sam Sheepdog and Ralph Wolf (Wile E. Coyote in another role) do simply what we all do: go to work each morning from their neighboring bungalows, and return home each evening after an eight-hour day; like all the rest of us, they only practice their trades at work.

"There are no judges, only men judging; no tramps, only men tramping . . ." So said Lewis Browne. And so it is with

145

Multitalented Daffy Duck as Robin Hood: ROBIN HOOD DAFFY *(1958)*

the wolf and sheepdog, and so it is with lions and elands on the Serengeti Plains; the lion's work hours are only when he's hungry; once he's satisfied, the predator and prey live peacefully together.

"Comedy is unusual people in real situations; farce is real people in unusual situations."

As an animation director I did not confuse myself with an effort to imitate Oscar Wilde or Bernard Shaw. Farce is not my biscuit. I felt then and I will always feel at home with Chaplin, with Keaton, with Laurel and Hardy and the great Harry Langdon, all unusual people trying to live, to eat, to love, engaged in the simple matter of survival in a complex world.

Within all of us dwells a Daffy Duck, a Donald Duck, an Elmer Fudd, a Coyote, a Sylvester, a Yosemite Sam. We try, and are usually able, to keep the more antisocial traits of those characters under control. If we want to live in reasonable peace with ourselves, we ruefully acknowledge them and do the best we can, with the full knowledge that occasionally the Grinch, Wile E. Coyote, or Daffy Duck will come piling to the surface and take over for a few seconds, a few minutes, or a few days or weeks.

Daffy as Dripalong Daffy: DRIPALONG DAFFY *(1951)— note brand from daughter's prep school, Quarter Circle V Bar Ranch School, later Orme School, near Mayer, Arizona*

The animation director and writer have an enormous advantage here, because we mine ourselves, dredge the Daffy in us to the surface, become Daffy, look at the world through Daffy's eyes, speak with Daffy's voice, move with Daffy's peculiar and unique musculature.

Knowing Daffy and *thinking* Daffy, we now ask ourselves a simple question: Where, as Daffy, am I? And how can I give that environment a slight, an ever so slight twist?

Being Daffy, I know that he would:

Daffy as disgusted hoofer— title footage from TV show

—Refuse to fly south (we would all like to be individualists). Title: Norm McCabe's *Daffy's Southern Exposure*

—Marry for money. There is a small pocket of avariciousness in all of us that whispers: Who wouldn't? Title: Friz Freleng's *His Bitter Half*

—Play Robin Hood and be unable to prove to anybody that he *is* Robin Hood. Title: My *Robin Hood Daffy*.

Robin Hood Daffy and Porky (Friar Tuck) Pig: ROBIN HOOD DAFFY *(1958)*

Wouldn't we all like to actually *be* the hero, not just dream about it, or, in this case, play *Buck Rogers*?

So this is where we got one of our ideas: *Daffy Duck as Buck Rogers*.

147

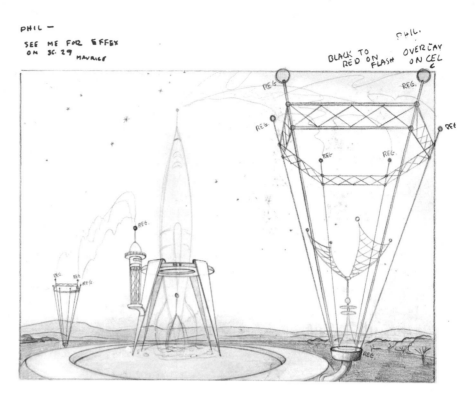

Maurice Noble's layout sketch for DUCK DODGERS IN THE 24½ CENTURY *(1953), designed ten years before any such craft had appeared at Cape Canaveral (or Kennedy)*

An idea has no worth at all without believable characters to implement it; a plot without characters is like a tennis court without players. Daffy Duck is to a Buck Rogers story what John McEnroe was to tennis.

Personality. That is the key, the drum, the fife. Forget the plot. Can you remember, or care to remember, the plot of any great comedy? Chaplin? Woody Allen? The Marx Brothers?

"[The writer] merely has some people in his mind, and an incident or two, also a locality. He knows the selected locality, and he trusts that he can plunge those people into incidents with interesting results."

— MARK TWAIN

All right. We now have a locality (the twenty-fifth century), an incident (the search for something), and some characters that interest us and, therefore, we hope, will interest an audience.

So let's get started.

First of all, we want a *title*. "First of all" only in terms of the finished picture; the title may appear at any time during pro-

Finished background by Phil De Guard

duction. Don't fight it, it will only slow you down. The title will appear.

The title should be honest and simple and, one hopes, to the point:*

Buck Rogers in the 25th Century
Duck Dodgers in the 24½ Century

Just as in the 1920s, *The Covered Wagon* was followed by a short comedy, *Two Wagons, Both Covered.*

LOCALITY: Far from imitating Buck Rogers, we go way beyond the clutching bonds of the earthbound live-action camera and what were then the miniature cities of the Future. We do this because we *can*, because we have that great and imaginative designer, Maurice Noble, to create a city of the future, a city that, even with today's advances in technology, still stands as the city to stimulate live-action directors such as George Lucas and Steven Spielberg.

Ten years before Cape Canaveral, Maurice also designed a forty-story rocket/spacecraft, complete with gantry never before seen by man. Wonderful!

149

* *The Coyote and Road Runner pictures were exceptions to this rule.*

THE INCIDENT: In science fiction, usually a quest for something is needed, something lost, something lifesaving. In our case, Mike Maltese and I realized that "the earth's supply of Illudium Phosdex, the shaving cream atom, is alarmingly low."

So now we have all we need to start a film. And here is how we went about it at Warner Bros.

1. THE IDEA: A loving parody of Buck Rogers.

2. THE CHARACTERS: Daffy and Porky and Marvin Martian and Dr. I.Q. High.

3. THE INCIDENT: The search for Illudium Phosdex.

4. THE ENVIRONMENT: Outer space and the city of the future.

I. STORY The writer and the director agree on the story idea or premise, and the writer (Mike Maltese) starts some rough storyboard sketches, ignoring continuity, concentrating on "business" between the characters. After about a week, the director calls a story session known as . . .

II. THE JAM SESSION—attended by three directors (Friz Freleng, Bob McKimson, and me), three writers (Warren Foster, Tedd Pierce, and Mike), and the production chief (Johnny Burton), and—often, sadly—the producer. (The layout men did not ordinarily attend the jam session. It was felt best to bring them in on completion of the storyboard, coincidentally working with the director as he does the character layouts.)

This session was, I believe, an event unique to Warner Bros. Unique at that time, perhaps anytime. Because this was not a brainstorming session in the usual sense, it was a "yes" session, not an "anything goes" session. Anything went, but only if it was positive, supportive, and affirmative to the premise. *No*

Johnny Burton, C. Martin Jones, and Friz Freleng, about 1958

*Anybody can crush an
infant idea with a cement "NO!"*

negatives were allowed. If you could not contribute, you kept quiet. For want of a better term, I have always called it . . .

THE "YES" SESSION. Again, the "yes" session is not a brainstorming session; repeat, it is not a session in which *anything goes.* The purpose is to advance an idea or ideas, not an emotional outburst for the emotional benefit of the participants or as a story man's confession of a buried affair with a girl's track shoe. The "yes" session only has one objective: to write a story.

The "yes" session imposes only one discipline: the abolition of the word "no." Anyone can say "no." It is the first word a child learns and often the first word he speaks. It is a cheap word because it requires no explanation, and many men and women have acquired a reputation for intelligence who know only this word and have used it in place of thought on every occasion. The "yes" session lasts only for two hours, but a person who can only say "no" finds it an eternity. Negative-minded people have been known to finally inflate and burst with accumulated negatives and say something positive, because it is also true that a person who heretofore can only say "no" is also a person who must say something.

A "no" is defined as any negative: "I don't like it." "There must be a better way." "I don't like to criticize, but . . ." "I've heard that one before." "I don't know." Or: "Oh, for Christ's sake, Chuck." All are roadblocks impeding the advancement and exploration of the value of an idea and are forbidden.

Of course, all story ideas are not good or useful, and if you find you cannot contribute, then silence is proper, but it is surprising how meaty and muscular a little old stringy "yes" (which is another name for a premise) can become in as little as fifteen or twenty minutes, when everyone present unreservedly commits his immediate impulsive and positive response to it. And, of course, the enlightened self-interest of

pouring your contributions unreservedly out in another director's story session is sufficient motivation; your turn will inevitably come to present an idea to the group in another session, and at such a time you, too, will want, need, and expect full cooperation. A good premise *always* generates the most astonishing results.

Following are notes taken at a jam session held December 13, 1949, for a film titled *Dripalong Daffy*:*

MUSIC: "HOME ON THE RANGE" AT OPENING TO ESTABLISH PEACE IN THE TOWN.

NAME OF TOWN: DONUT CENTER. COMMENT WRITTEN ON SIGN: "WHAT A HOLE!"

CLOTHING-STORE DUMMY HOLDING UP CIGAR-STORE INDIAN.

DAFFY DIGS THROUGH AN ASSORTMENT OF BADGES, FINDS ONE MARKED "SHERIFF," AND PINS IT ON HIMSELF. LOOKS AGAIN AND FINDS A DEPUTY'S BADGE, AND PINS IT ON PORKY.

BANDIT CHANGES ASSETS ON THE BANK WINDOW.

WHEN DAFFY PINS ON HIS SHERIFF'S BADGE, HE FLIPS UP SIGN SAYING: "SHERIFF WANTED." ANOTHER SIGN FLIPS DOWN SAYING: "YOU FOOL YOU!"

LABELS ON BOTTLES: FOREST LAWN DEW
                        CEMETERY DEW
                        RADIOACTIVE RYE

AFTER NASTY CANASTA SHOOTS THE MILK SHAKE OUT OF DAFFY'S HAND HE WALKS AWAY, LEAVING THE SIGN WITH HIS PICTURE IN VIEW.

152

* *The notes on* Duck Dodgers *are in some forgotten limbo.*

DAFFY SHOVES GUN DOWN CANASTA'S THROAT RIGHT UP TO THE TRIGGER. CANASTA CHEWS IT OFF TO THE CYLINDER, LEAVING GUNPOWDER DRIPPING OUT.

ELIMINATE THE CHASER AFTER CANASTA DRINKS HIS DRINK. CUT OUT: "I'M GONNA FREEZE YOUR DECK."

TO ESTABLISH THE STRENGTH OF THE DRINK, CANASTA DRINKS IT AND THE GLASS MELTS.

AFTER DOWNING THE DRINK, DAFFY FALLS THROUGH A HOLE IN THE FLOOR, THEN COMES SHOOTING OUT, WITH ROCKETS SHOOTING OUT AFTER HIM.

CANASTA LIGHTS UP CIGARETTE JUST BY BLOWING ON IT.

CANASTA'S BREATH COMES OUT IN MUSHROOM-LIKE SPURTS AFTER DRINKING DRINK.

BARTENDER PUTS ON WELDER'S MASK AND HEAVY GLOVES WHILE HE MIXES DRINK WITH A RIVETING MACHINE.

CANASTA'S HAT FLIPS UP AS HE DOWNS DRINK.

CANASTA SUGGESTS RUSSIAN ROULETTE.

PORKY WINDS UP A TOY SOLDIER. IT WALKS ACROSS CANASTA'S PATH, HE PICKS IT UP, IT GOES THROUGH MANEUVERS, CANASTA LAUGHS, SOLDIER AIMS GUN AT CANASTA AND SHOOTS HIM.

DAFFY: "I'M GOING TO CLEAN UP THIS ONE-HORSE TOWN."
PORKY: "LUCKY FOR HIM IT'S A ONE-HORSE TOWN!"

My layout sketches from
DRIPALONG DAFFY (1951)

Question: But what if nothing happens? What if the premise just lies doggo with faint response or no response at all from anybody?

Answer: The director will know, not because there is silence, but by the quality of the response; if the suggestions are un-

Rough background for DUCK DODGERS IN THE 24½ CENTURY (1953)

responsive to the basic idea, if the others are floundering, the director will know within a half hour and will gracefully excuse everyone. Either the presentation is wrong or the idea is wrong. Since we trust each other, we will accept the situation not as a rebuff but as a mute, implicit suggestion that "we *want* to be turned on, but this is not working."

So we try again.

In each case the moderator is the director who has asked for the meeting. It is his sole judgment as to what is negative and there can be no protest at the end of the session. All comments and criticism are welcome if the moderator desires and asks for them, but usually they have all occurred to him during the course of the discussion and he prefers to contemplate his notes before he decides on the disciplines and restrictions needed. Weariness and impracticalities nearly always surface without the help of the ubiquitous "no" sayers. This method has been adopted by many groups, and I have never heard of it failing where these simple rules were observed.

III. THE STORYBOARD   There was never a script at Warner Bros. All stories we developed on rough storyboards. Approximately 150 rough story sketches and rough dialogue were needed for a six-minute cartoon (540 film feet: 1½ feet or 24 frames equals one second). The writer—in my case, Mike Maltese—had five weeks, working with the director, to outline in sketches a six-minute cartoon storyboard.

After the board is completed, another story session is held, but this is brief and to the point, to see if there are any obvious errors in structure, dialogue, or character. The storyboard is then turned over to the director.

154

IV. DIRECTION   The story as it will eventually appear on the screen is now less than half done. We are at the point where the live-action director, script in hand, would step onto the sound stage, but unlike the live-action director, the animation director cannot tell his actors what to do—whips or gentle persuasion are equally useless when dealing with drawings.

Background men are a separate breed: Paul Julian, 1942

A. *Character and Background Layout.* The director now draws about 300 key poses or character layouts for each six-minute cartoon. This is *not* animation; the drawings are a guide to facial expression, posture, size, physical and mental attitudes, and relations to one another. At the same time he is staging the characters in individual scenes, or rough backgrounds corresponding to sets in live action. As he is laying out the film, he will find the number of individual backgrounds that will be needed for this particular picture: fifty-five to sixty on *Duck Dodgers* to over a hundred on *What's Opera, Doc?* Before starting the character layouts, however, the director calls in his background designer (background layout man), in this case the

155

talented Maurice Noble, and goes over the story as it was brought to him. The director, if he is me, then instructs Maurice to ignore me and search the storyboard for graphic ideas and staging possibilities. These are known as inspirational sketches. On pictures like *Duck Dodgers* this creative input is a must for me and for the picture. Maurice was largely responsible for the grand opening sequences of this film, plus ideas such as the enormous scanning eye, the vaporizers, and the wonderfully exact rocket. Maurice reported back in about a week with the sheaf of superb little sketches I would find so useful as I completed the character layout drawings for the rest of the film.

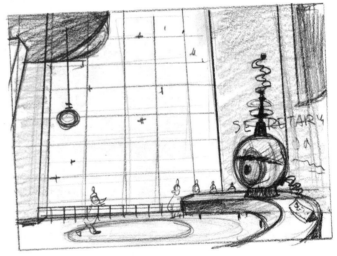

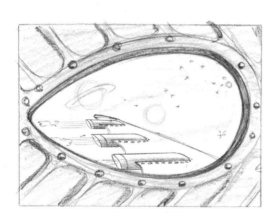

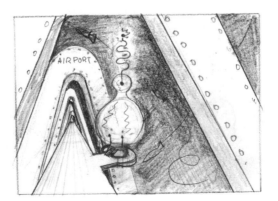

More inspirational sketches by Maurice Noble for DUCK DODGERS IN THE 24½ CENTURY *(1953)*

156

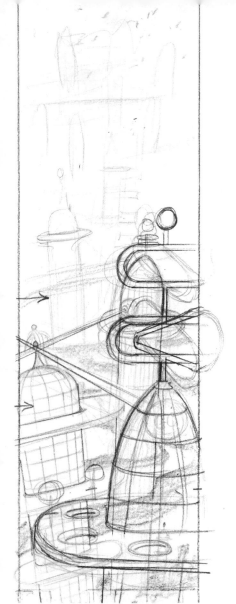

MAURICE NOBLE
(Layout)

If a lawyer who defends himself in court has a fool for a client, then a director who tries to act as his own background layout man is doomed to a kind of spasticity, handicapped by his own limitations. It is not only necessary that he hire a layout man of talent superior to his own; he must demand that such a person approach the same filmic problem with a different history and viewpoint. For myself, I do not want a layout man who thinks he is a director, but I do want him to have the confidence, and the knowledge, to know that I consider him far better at his job than I ever could be.

Maurice seldom tried to provide animation gags per se, but he created a world where animation could flourish. If, for instance, in *What's Opera, Doc?* he felt the lack of flesh tones and frippery common to classic ballet, he designed the backgrounds in flesh tones and the trees as tutus. If, as in one of the Martian outer-space films, he got tired of all those cinematically overdone mysterious planets, he simply designed a city of delicately hued transparent plates floating in space. In *Duck Dodgers in the 24½ Century* Maurice designed a forty-story rocket ten years before John Glenn graduated from high school, and vastly superior in design to anything seen at the Kennedy Space Center, or anywhere else. Maurice's visual jokes, however, never intruded on the orderly advance of the story—if any story I ever directed could be called orderly.

He enhanced every story. He stimulated all who worked with him. He always used the concerto form: once he was familiar with the story intent, every inspirational sketch he contributed before I started to lay the characters out was a variation on

Duck Dodgers and supervideo detecto set

Marvin Martian's ultimate weapon

Noble designs

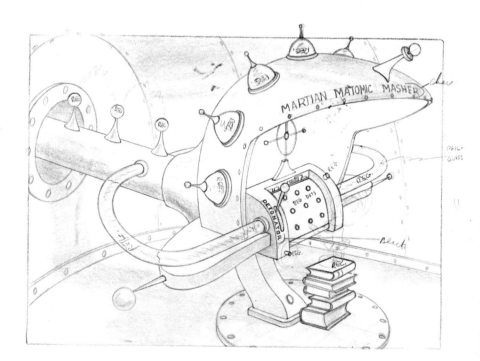

the theme. He never showed off, but he showed up every layout man I have ever known by his honesty, his devotion to his craft, and, above all, his devotion to the film at hand, and this is nowhere more vividly demonstrated than in *What's Opera, Doc?* Without Maurice Noble, who excited, moved, and stimulated us all, a great many of my films could not have been made.

As the scientist said to Daffy in *Duck Dodgers*, I said to Maurice: "I have sent for you, Dodgers, because the world supply of great layout men is appallingly low."*

PHIL DE GUARD

If Maurice Noble was the architect of our films, Phil De Guard was the master builder. He took Maurice's inspirational sketches and structural blueprints and fashioned them into graceful reality. He enhanced the believability of the characters who moved across and through his sets. By his craftsmanship he could simulate two-dimensional backgrounds as needed in *The Dot and the Line* or achieve depth by a series of diminishing flats as subtle as a Japanese print. Don Graham, arguably the greatest teacher animation ever knew or would ever know, described this remarkable effect in the Road Runner films as "pure mass moving, perhaps for the first time, in pure space." I am sure Phil would have been astonished at such remarkable praise from such a respected source, but it is seldom noticed even by erudite critics that, except for the necessary diminishing roads, he had little use for a vanishing point. The movement of the Coyote and the Road Runner into the distance provided all the proof necessary that we were indeed dealing in deep space. If Maurice and Phil had taken the time to describe in justifying detail what they were doing on the Road Runner

* This is as good a time as any to bend a grateful knee to designer Liney Li, who, through patience, artistry, and wisdom, somehow managed to make a recognizable quilt out of these patches.

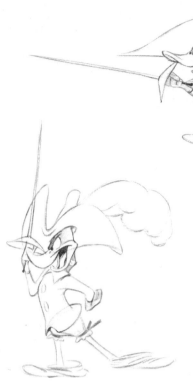

The gallant opening with Daffy (D'Artagnan) Duck: DUCK AMUCK (1953)

films, I probably would have been alarmed at their revolutionary effrontery and forbidden it. But I, too, was so bedazzled by the result that I had no trouble accepting it, and doubtless I would have taken credit for it if I had known what they were so successfully doing.

Phil was a quiet and gentle man: talent, technique, creativity, and honesty were all his, without the necessity for comment. He was without doubt among the finest of my contemporaries in filmmaking, a man devoted to the common good. I would have been lost without him.

B. The director lays the picture out by drawing the aforesaid 300 character sketches on animation paper.

He soon learns to start from a sequence that interests him most, working forward and back, seldom from the beginning of the film. Once I directed an entire cartoon by stumbling on the phrase "Ascent of the Matterhorn" and realizing that if "ascent" became "a scent," the title *A Scent of the Matterhorn* would be a perfectly natural vehicle for Pepé Le Pew, the little French skunk. The story fell together with amazing ease, as though it were self-storyboarded, which indeed it was, since I went directly into layout from the title.

This seldom happened. I seldom knew the end of the story when I started on it, and sometimes even a satisfactory beginning eluded me: the Bugs Bunny ending in *Duck Amuck* was not discovered until the last week of layout; the opening of *The Scarlet Pumpernickel* came after the film was half laid out.

Both Mike Maltese and I were devoted devotees of the cloak-and-dagger genre. From Fairbanks, Alaska, to Hollywood, California, is several thousand miles, but from Fairbanks (Doug) to Flynn (Errol) is only the difference in the length of a rapier blade. Our life spans comfortably encompassed the great precursor, Fairbanks, and his swashbuckling descendant, Flynn.

It looks as if a world so elegantly created would have a chance of survival, n'est-ce pas?

The hope of man- and duck-kind rides with D. Dodgers

Maurice's depiction of Planet X.
If it were Armageddon, Porky would
be saying, "Ah-ah-ah-'m-geddin' outta here!"

My wise wife Marian believes that somebody just as idiotic as Daffy may have his nervous hand on just such a believable lever

It only takes one

Finished model of a finishing weapon

Marvin Martian and fair but unacceptable
offer of terms from Duck Dodgers

One of those delicate misunderstandings
which often lead to serious consequences

*Daffy (Duck Dodgers)
Duck: "I claim this
planet in the name of
the Earth!"*

*Note that the "bit of dirt"
that Daffy is now
claiming for the Earth is
about the size of a moth-
eaten plum pudding*

*... and Porky wisely puts
the whole picture and
perhaps the whole world
into perspective: "B-big
deal!"*

It was therefore inevitable that we would eventually try to demonstrate everything we knew and loved about adventure films in one six-minute cartoon, *The Scarlet Pumpernickel*. Just as we would later take the entire fourteen hours of *The Ring of the Nibelung* and squash it down to the six-minute *What's Opera, Doc?*

This drama had to star Daffy Duck, because he, more than any other of our characters, aspired to be Flynn's successor. So we started storyboarding all the lovely clichés characteristic of the Three Musketeers, Robin Hood, Captain Blood film form. Without really worrying too much about structure. Then one day we were startled to see that Daffy was *succeeding*—something he had never done before, and for good reason: Daffy's entire persona is based on lack of success. He is a companion of Laurel and Hardy, Woody Allen, Buster Keaton. How could we let him succeed and fail at the same time?

Mike came up with the solution: Daffy is telling the story, narrating it to someone.

Who?

Why not Jack Warner, the paragon of creative encouragement. Why not just call him J.L.? We were safe there: Jack, on seeing the film, would never recognize himself beneath so obscure a pseudonym.

So it grew. The fruit was there, now we needed a believable shell. It became obvious. Daffy is sick of playing comedy. As he puts it, "Ah-ha, hoo-hoo, yuck-yuck, always comedy, ya just gotta give me a chance, J.L.!"

And so it went, occasionally flipping back to Daffy, the script-writer putting more and more heaving-ho into his telling to the unresponsive J.L. Finally, in an agony of frustration and chagrin, Daffy shoots himself through the beret, only to sit up with a last despairing remark, "Ya gotta kill yourself to sell a script around here."

DASHING THROUGH THE
STINSON (FOSTER) YAH HAH HAH
IN A ONE HORSE OPEN SLEIGH..
THROUGH THE FIELDS WE GO

Daffy trying to adjust:
DUCK AMUCK (1953)

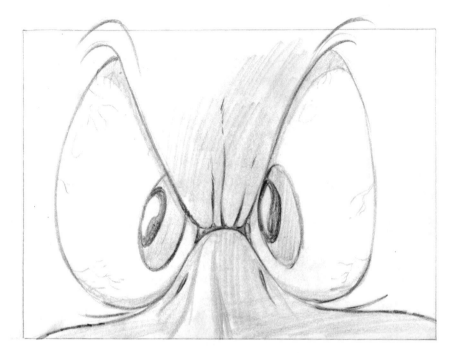

"This is a close-up?"

Maurice baffled Daffy with this background

170

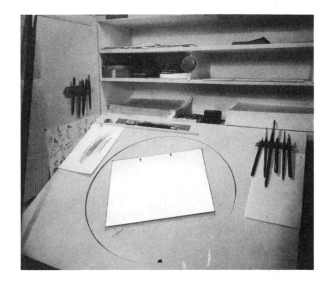

"Ain't I a stinker?"

Bugs's drawing board finale: DUCK AMUCK *(1953)*

When the ending came about in *Duck Amuck*, it was as a practical solution rather than a creative one. *Duck Amuck* happened almost exclusively on the drawing board as I drew, laid out, the key character poses and wrote the dialogue. Monologue actually, since Daffy was the only voice heard. Mike worked at my shoulder on this one, rather than on a storyboard. From the first scene, when Daffy leaps out, saber in hand, shouting, "Stand back, Musketeers—they shall sample *my* blade," to the penultimate ("next to last," I believe) scene, where Daffy is shouting in absolute frustration, "Who *are* you; I demand that you show yourself!!" he has been in conflict with the animator who is drawing him—in a word: me. Who else could it be? With Mike's help, I had to meet each succeeding contretemps as it occurred, fighting our way out of one of Daffy's frustrations after another. But what now? I couldn't appear on the screen even if I was the opponent. There was only one person in the whole world who had known equal conflict with Daffy Duck. In *Duck! Rabbit! Duck!, Rabbit Seasoning, Ali Baba Bunny,* and others, he and only he knew how to deal with Daffy. So I simply pulled the camera back to find Bugs at the drawing board. He turns to the audience and, perhaps tickled, but a little ashamed, says, "Ain't I a stinker?" It was the only ending possible.

c. *Dialogue*. During the growth and completion of the story-board, tentative dialogue was written beneath the story sketches. The final, complete dialogue always waited until the director had finished the 300 to 400 key sketches called character layout drawings.

Few screenwriters can write action and few story men can draw finished action poses. At Warner Bros., all finished action and all finished dialogue were fashioned by the director.

Only after the layouts and therefore the dialogue were complete did I simply hand the sketches over to a secretary, who put the dialogue onto dialogue sheets for the actors.

DUCK DODGERS IN THE 24½ CENTURY   1953

Writer: Mike Maltese   PRODUCTION NO. 1264

1. DOCTOR: I have sent for you, Dodgers, because we are facing a crisis. The world supply of Illudium Phosdex, the shaving cream atom, is alarmingly low . . .

2. DOCTOR: Now we have reason to believe that the only remaining source is on Planet X . . . somewhere in *this* area . . .

3. DAFFY: . . . And you want *me* to find Planet X, eh?

4. DOCTOR: Can you do it, Dodgers?

5. DAFFY: Indubitibutly, sir . . . 'cause there's no one knows his way around outer space like . . . *Duck Dodgers, in the twenty-fourth and a half century!!!*

6. DAFFY: Are you ready, eager young space cadet?

7. PORKY: I'm r-r-re, r-r-read . . . all s-set, your heroship, sir!

8. DAFFY: Then make way for . . . *Duck Dodgers, in the twenty-fourth and a half century!!*

9. DAFFY: (Embarrassed) *Oops!* Had the silly thing in reverse!

10. DAFFY: Hello, calling Planet Earth! 3XAL calling . . . Hello . . . Hello . . .

11. DAFFY: Hey, that you, Earth? We have just passed the Dog Star at two million miles and shifting into second . . . and putting her in automatic pilot.

12. DAFFY: Jumping Jupiter going by now . . . Am putting her into automatic pilot.
[These last lines (10, 11, 12) were taken out before animation]

13. DAFFY: And now then, eager young space cadet, here is the course we shall pursue to find Planet X . . .

14. DAFFY: Starting from where we are, we go 33,600

turbo miles due up . . . Then west in an astro-arc deviation to here . . . then following the great circle seven radiolubes south by down-east . . . by astro-astrolabe to here . . . here . . . and here . . . then by space-navigo compass to here . . . here . . . then to here . . . and here . . . by thirteen point strato-cumulus bear-ing four million light-years . . . and thus to our destination.

15.	DAFFY:	*Now* do you know how to reach Planet X?
16.	PORKY:	Y-y-yessir!
17.	DAFFY:	Well, I wish you'd explain it to me sometime, buster!
18.	PORKY:	Why, it's very simple, sir, if we follow *those planets* we can't very well miss Planet X . . .
19.	DAFFY:	*Haw! Haw! Haw!* That's ridiculous! Of all the stupid suggestions . . . Ah, ha ha ha ha! Wait a minute . . . I think I've got it . . . I'll just bet that if we follow *those* planets we'll find Planet X!!
20.	DAFFY:	Gad, how do I do it?
21.	PORKY:	(Admiringly) I d-don't know!

22. DAFFY: *I CLAIM THIS PLANET IN THE NAME OF THE EARTH!!*

23. MARTIAN: I claim this planet in the name of Mars!! Isn't that lovely?

24. DAFFY: Look, bud . . . I've got news for you . . . I have already claimed this bit of dirt for the Earth and there just ain't room enough on this planet for the two of us!

25. MARTIAN: I do believe you are right. Yes.

26. DAFFY: Little does he realize that I have on my disintegration-proof vest.

27. DAFFY: You may fire when ready, Grisly . . .

28. DAFFY: *Who? What? Where? When? How? Who?* Oh, *you,* eh? Just when I had him going, you hadda butt in!! Well, get back in that spaceship!!

Master shot of Planet X:
DUCK DODGERS IN THE 24½
CENTURY (1953)

29.	PORKY:	Yessir . . . your heroship!!
30.	DAFFY:	Brother . . . the things I have to put up with . . .
31.	DAFFY:	(Triumphant) Ah ha!!! Got the drop on ya with *my* disintegrating pistol!!
32.	DAFFY:	And, brother, when it disintegrates, it disintegrates!
33.	DAFFY:	(Sheepishly) Well . . . whaddaya know . . . it disintegrated . . .
34.	PORKY:	H-happy birthday . . . you thing from another world, you . . .
35.	MARTIAN:	Oh, thank you.
36.	MARTIAN:	Now, how do you suppose he knew it was my birthday? Especially when it isn't?
37.	DAFFY:	Well, I guess he's had enough. I'll send him an ultimatum.

38.	DAFFY:	I'll see what the little stinker is up to on my supervideo detecto set.
39.	DAFFY:	(Hysterically angry) *That's the last straw . . . NOW I USE MY SECRET WEAPON!!!*
40.	DAFFY:	(Dirty laugh . . . crescendo)
41.	MARTIAN:	(Dirty laugh) (Shorter)
42.	DAFFY:	As I was saying, buster, this planet ain't big enough for the two of us so . . . *off you go!!*
43.	DAFFY:	And now . . . This planet is hereby claimed for the Earth in the name of . . . *Duck Dodgers in the twenty-fourth and a half century!!*
44.	PORKY:	B-big deal!

D. *Recording.* The actor or actors were called into a prearranged dialogue room or sound stage, where the director went over the sketches with the voice-over actor, usually the highly talented and versatile Mel Blanc, who did Bugs, Daffy, Porky, Tweety, Yosemite Sam, Sylvester, and most of the others, except female voices, which were done by the equally talented June Foray.

Since some of the voices were speeded up to give them a quicker and higher quality (e.g., those of Porky, Tweety, and Daffy) and as Mel cannot be expected to talk convincingly to himself, we recorded one voice at a time. On the first recording I would be Daffy to his Porky, and each line was repeated as many times as necessary to get the intonation needed by the director.

It must be emphasized that the director must have the exact emphasis, timing, and character thoroughly in mind. The off-stage actor does *not* improvise unless asked to by the director. For example, in one of the Duck Season/Rabbit Season films, Daffy, in an agony of frustration, crawls his way to Bugs, takes him by the shirt front, and blurts *"You're dethpicable!"* This is not the end of the film, so we cannot conveniently iris out—so what does Daffy say now, in that absolute frustration, as Bugs turns calmly and saunters away? Daffy follows him, but he has lost all ability to insult, accuse, or shame Bugs; he has also lost his vocabulary. Explaining this situation to Mel, I said, "Daffy has forgotten every word in the English language but 'dethpicable'—so you can use any epithet you like, as long as it's 'dethpicable.' " And Mel blurted out: "Yeth, you're dethpicable, and not only that, you're picable and deth, deth; in all the years I've been in thith business, I've never met anyone so picable!" It required several takes and suggestions, but it was well worth it.

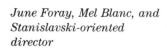

June Foray, Mel Blanc, and Stanislavski-oriented director

E. *Dialogue Reading.* The audio part of the film—or sound track—is then processed (no tape then), and the director selects the proper takes, which are then spliced together and presented for his final approval.

The editor then puts the sound track on a Moviola and runs

it through, listening to the sound in slow motion (this is impossible, so don't ask me how he did it). And separating the consonants from the vowels, indicating "uhs," inhales, and grunts as well as the words, he transfers the sounds to dialogue sheets.

F. *Timing the Film.* The director then brings the dialogue, background, layouts, and penciled characters together.

What happens now requires a moment of history. In the early 1930s, wages were very low and it did not matter much whether a cartoon ran seven or eight minutes. But as demand grew for them, salaries increased, and it became evident even to knuckleheads like our producers that shortening the length of a film would decrease the cost.

. . . I am sure our producer, Leon Schlesinger, would have shortened films to two minutes had he not encountered an opponent he could not contravene: the exhibitor, who demanded that *any* short subject be no shorter than six minutes, to round out a two-hour program composed of a feature, a trailer (preview), a newsreel, and a short subject (preferably a cartoon, since they made people laugh—a nice commodity).

Well, Leon knew what his next course would be. By God, if they couldn't be any shorter than six minutes, they sure as hell weren't going to be any longer.

So, as a matter of survival rather than artistry, the directors at Warners soon learned to time a picture to exactly six minutes (540 feet).

From the beginning of the idea, then, until the final film, the director had to keep always in his mind: six minutes, no more, no less.

Now, to the horror of directors like Spielberg, Scorsese, Lucas, Wise, and so on, these cartoons had to be timed exactly to six minutes *before* they were given to the animators, before ink and paint, camera, and finished sound and picture. I believe this exact discipline was unique to Warner Bros., and certainly it increased our respect for and love of precise timing. (Always at Disney, and to a certain extent at M-G-M, editing was not only allowed but expected, and length could vary by as much as a minute.)

. . . Each scene cut, each step, each phoneme of dialogue, each hand movement, bite, explosion, laugh, was meticulously timed to the twenty-fourth of a second, each of five thousand drawings accounted for, each piece of action carefully planned and timed. The director is the composer.

V. ANIMATION   ANIMATE: [*Webster's*] From Latin, *animatus*— to invoke life, to make alive, to give life to, bring to life, to stimulate to action or creative effort.

ANIMATION: **"Animation is not the art of drawings that move, but the art of movements that are drawn."**

— NORMAN MC LAREN

Animation could therefore apply to all spoken drama, from *Lysistrata* through *King Lear, Waiting for Godot*, to Chaplin, Keaton, and us.

What we did at Warner Bros. is often called "character animation," but if one considers Webster, this is redundant. Indeed, there are many other forms of movement done under a flatbed camera, called, wisely, "film graphics."

The surprising and largely unnoticed thing about animation is that it does not require a camera. It exists in the finished scene. The sheaf of drawings can be held in your hand and flipped for a very small audience—as many as can look over your shoulder, the way it had been done by children for years before the advent of the motion-picture camera.

It is not known how far back in history flipping goes—perhaps back to the first book, so it seems obvious that the first time an inquisitive child got hold of a book, flipping or animation was invented.

Animation is acting and an animator must respond to the same exacting disciplines as an actor does.

The animator must, in short, be able to perform on a bare stage, without words, without settings, without music, and be understood, and that is precisely what we did at Warners. Upon completion of animation, and without any of the aforesaid elements, we ran the pencil or line test, silent, to see if it worked on that bare stage. This was as true of a verbose character like Pepé Le Pew or Bugs Bunny as it was of mute characters like the Coyote and Road Runner. You can prove the vitality of this kind of animation to yourself: on Saturday morning, turn off the sound of the Bugs Bunny show and note that you can tell pretty much what is happening.

Full animation *is* acting. Just as the actor demonstrates a part *not* by what he looks like but by *how* he moves, so the animator takes simple graphics and brings them to life in the *way* they move and by the intricate timing necessary to achieve that life.

Limited animation   *Full animation*

Storyboard:
HOW TO MAKE AN ANIMATED CARTOON

Starring
Daffy
(Alistair)
Duck

1. Daffy: "The making of an animated cartoon is absurdly simple . . ."

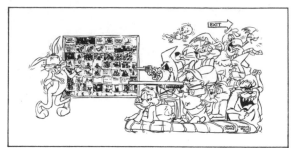

2. Daffy: ". . . all one must do is obtain the enthusiastic cooperation and unselfish input from one's colleagues."

3. Daffy: "Then one only needs to proceed to the sound stage and shoot the film."

4. Daffy: "As said, it is so absurdly simple that even a child could do . . ."

5. Daffy: ". . . it."

6. Bugs: "Well, maybe not that simple. Even in the beginning animation was pretty complicated . . . in fact, in one of the very first animated cartoons, GERTIE THE DINOSAUR . . ."

7. Bugs: ". . . the great animator Winsor McKay had to draw the entire background scene for every fraction of a second . . ."

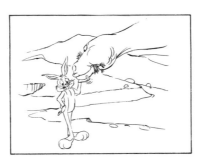

8. Bugs: ". . . as well as drawing all those Gerties. Now, that was way back in 1914, probably before you were born."

9. Bugs: "Then someone developed a material called celluloid ('cel'), and we didn't have to draw the background over and over again, twenty-four times a second."

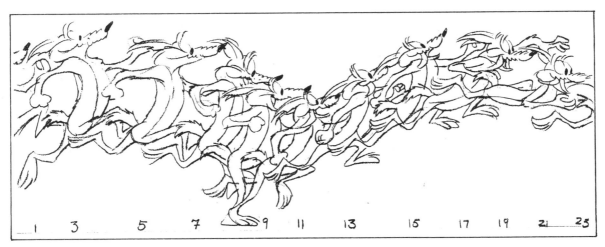

10. Bugs: "Yes, that's how many there are in full animation: twelve to twenty-four individual drawings each second."

11. Bugs: "The animator's pencil drawings are transferred to the cel, either by hand inking or by a form of phototransfer."

12. Bugs: "The reverse side of the cel is then painted with, in this case, coyote colors."

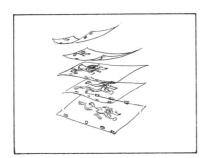

13. Bugs: "Then we place in sequence as many cels as the action requires over the same background painting."

14. Bugs: "The cels and the background painting are laid under heavy glass under air pressure and photographed one twenty-fourth of a second at a time."

15. Bugs: "And that's really all there is to it . . ."

16. Elmer: "Except for a few small details, wike witing the stowy . . ."

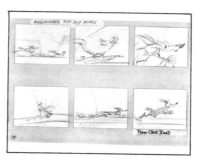

17. Elmer: "After all, the witer and diwector have to devewop the stowyboard . . . and decide what the Woad Wunner and Coyote are going to do next . . ."

18. Bugs chimes in: "Well, directors do have to earn their living somehow . . . like working with the music department to decide on the tempo and orchestration . . ."

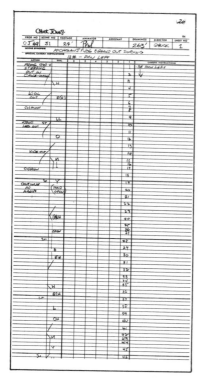

19. Bugs: "And the dialogue is transferred to exposure sheets by (guess who?) . . . the director."

20. Bugs: "In his spare time the director does three or four hundred character layout sketches for each film to help animators understand the action he wants."

21. Bugs: "And just to be sure that everybody will draw the characters the same way, he also must draw model sheets of each character."

22. Bugs: "Meanwhile the scenic designer (or layout person) is designing the backgrounds for the guidance of the animators."

23. Bugs: "The animators make the key pencil drawings called 'extremes.' A good animator at Warner Bros. could do about fifteen seconds of film time a week."

184

24. Bugs: "With the help of the assistant animator (or 'in-betweener'), who, surprisingly enough, puts drawings in between the animator's 'extremes.'"

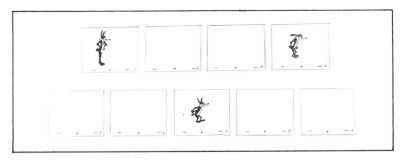

25. Bugs: "As you can see, the assistant animator must be a highly-trained artist, too."

26. Bugs: "The drawings then go to the 'ink and paint' department, where (to nobody's surprise) they are inked and painted."

27. Bugs: "Then the cels are delivered to the camera room . . . all five thousand to six thousand of them . . ."

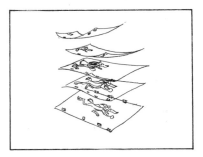

28. Bugs: "They float down onto the camera . . . well, they don't exactly float . . ."

29. Bugs: "Actually, every one of those five or six thousand cels must be carefully placed and photographed, one at a time, correctly, over the backgrounds."

30. Bugs: "Then it's just a matter of mixing the picture, the music, the dialogue, and the sound effects together and you have a six-minute animated cartoon."

31. Porky: "That's all, Folks!"

MY PAW!

Harris, Levitow, Thompson, Washam, Monroe & Vaughan

Not a law firm, but artists who firmly believed in the pleasure of their craft and the joy of animation.

Ken Harris, who could equally well animate the most outrageous Father's Day celebration ever in *A Bear for Punishment* or the results of a coyote overdosed on earthquake pills in *Hopalong Casualty* or the ballet sequence in *What's Opera, Doc?*

Abe Levitow, who animated the wonderfully hilarious laughing scene in *Robin Hood Daffy*, with Porky Pig as Friar Tuck, and who also found no difficulty in transforming the fearsome Nasty Canasta in *Barbary Coast Bunny* into a sort of human steamroller who could also have cast the gigantic shadows in the Night-on-Bald-Mountain sequence in *What's Opera, Doc?*

Richard Thompson, whose specialty, among many others,

Michael Maltese, coach . . . and the indomitable volleyball team from Pimento University: Monroe, Washam, Levitow, Thompson, and Harris

was Sam Sheepdog, in *A Sheep in the Deep* and others, as well
as Daffy's fight sequence with the Shropshire Slasher in *Deduce,
You Say*.

Ben Washam, master of animation, sensitive delineator of
Ralph Phillips, the daydreaming little boy in *From A to
Z-Z-Z-Z*, and master, too, of Pepé Le Pew in *For Scent-imental
Reasons* and the flying kitten in *Go Fly a Kit*.

Phil Monroe, who worked so hard in my early years to make
me a decent director. His Bugs Bunny in *Super-Rabbit, Case
of the Missing Hare, Frigid Hare*, and *Long-Haired Hare* helped
me at last to understand the inner workings of Bugs's brain.

Lloyd Vaughan, whose interest and artistry in *everything* in
animation from a wayward flame to a mysterious Mynah Bird,
from a lightning strike to an eighteen-foot Elmer in *Beanstalk
Bunny* were both a wonder and a life-ring to me.

I am grateful beyond words to have had these wonderful men
to guide my stumbling footsteps along the road to a reasonable
competence.

Yes, Mahatma Gandhi wasn't kidding when he said: "There
they go. I must run and catch up with them, because I am their
leader!" So I ran to catch up with my animators, and maybe I
grew up a little under their unconscious tutelage.

If, as Ed Wynn said, a comedian is not a person who opens
a funny door but a person who opens a door funny, then these
men were comedians through the art form we call animation.

Harris by Harris   *Levitow by Levitow*   *Thompson by Thompson*

VI. ASSISTANT ANIMATION (OR IN-BETWEENS)   The animator does the key drawings, working over a light board, from the director's character layouts and the exposure sheets. Unlike other forms of graphic arts, the individual drawing has little meaning. We are dealing here with a flurry of drawings flipped before your eyes. Each drawing is on the screen $\frac{1}{24}$ of a second, far too fast for the human eye, whose visual receptivity of a single drawing is about one-tenth of a second.

The animator may do drawings 1, 4, 7, 9, 13, 14, 15, and 20—depending on the delicacy or breadth of the action.

The assistant animator, once called an in-betweener, places two of the animator's drawings, called "extremes," over the light board and literally in-betweens them, finding number 2 between 1 and 3, or drawings 5, 6, and 7 between drawings 4 and 8. And so on, for four thousand to five thousand drawings.

Consistency of the characters is assured by use of "model sheets" as well as the director's character layouts.

As each scene is completed, it is first flipped by the animator and the director, then set for a pencil or line test shot under the animation camera, without backgrounds or color. It is then spliced into a loop and viewed over and over again by the animator, the director, and the assistant, to detect any misplaced drawings, whether the action works correctly, and how it relates to the scenes that precede and follow.

At the conclusion of animation, all these loops are spliced together like a test pencil reel and viewed again for continuity, timing, and animation errors. Only then is it considered ready for ink and paint.

VII. MUSIC AND SOUND EFFECTS   When the animated cartoon is completed to the director's satisfaction in test (pencil reel) form (that is, without backgrounds, color, dialogue, music, voices, or sound added), then, as the several thousand cels go

to be inked and painted, the exposure sheets and the film go to the composer and the sound-effects editor.

CARL STALLING
(Music)

Carl Stalling, after a caricature by Tee Hee

Carl's beginnings in show business were as an organist in one of the big theaters in Kansas City (the Majestic?). In the silent-film days, a musical score was written to accompany the film when it went into distribution, to be played by the theater organist or, in some cases, a full orchestra.

Sometimes the score failed to arrive, and this is how Carl Stalling came to be the finest and most competent musician in animation. In those instances when the score didn't arrive, the organist, after perhaps one rehearsal, would have to improvise

music to fit the film, which could be anything from *The Great Train Robbery* to *Broken Blossoms* to Chaplin's *Shoulder Arms* to *The Prisoner of Zenda*. Carl amassed over those frustrating years perhaps the most comprehensive musical encyclopedia ever to be inculcated into a human brain.

When he accompanied Walt Disney west, he provided the score for all the early Disney talking films: *Steamboat Willie, Flowers and Trees, The Skeleton Dance*, etc. By great good luck, we at Warners inherited him in the middle 1930s, and what a jewel he was. And what a wizard. He could and often did write the score for an animated cartoon in five days, to be followed by Milt Franklin's brilliant arrangements. They were both equally familiar with contemporary and classical music. Carl was a joy, another section of the creative glue that made our little card house stable.

Tregoweth Brown—the greatest sound editor in films; Academy Award for THE GREAT RACE

TREG BROWN
(Sound Effects)

Treg had been a coal miner, a college student (unusual in those days), guitarist and vocalist for Red Nichols and His Five Pennies, hobo and tramp,* songwriter, graduate chiropractor, Rosicrucian, linguist,† Academy Award winner,‡ and finally a resident Catholic in Spain. We once asked him, if he had it to do over again, would he do it the same way. After a moment's thought he replied, "I don't think so, I wouldn't have the time."

But as sound-effects editor is where he shined. He could contrive more sound effects with an inflated balloon (earth-

* *There is a difference: hoboes are willing to work.*
† *Spanish and, I think, Urdu.*
‡ *Sound effects on* The Great Race.

Moral: Don't use glue
on a dynamite stick

quakes, wrestling grunts and groans, branches breaking, bull-frogs croaking, etc., etc.) than most editors could with all the sound devices at their command. With a newspaper, Treg could create any kind of fire from bon- to forest to rocket.

But it was as a master of incongruity in the Road Runner and Coyote and other films that he was at his resonant best. He realized that if the eye saw one thing and the ear heard another, subconsciously aroused laughter could result. As an example, but a good one, in one sequence when the Coyote got his foot caught in the line attached to a harpoon and was dragged willy-nilly across the desert floor over cacti, under boulders, bumping and slapping every obstacle possible, never once did Treg supply a logical sound effect: flying springs, breaking bottles, small explosives, human ouch'es and oof's, popping balloons, railroad crossing bells, and so on.

He was a jewel, was Treg. He added laughter where mild ha-ha's might have served. He served us well indeed, and he closed the ranks as the final creative good soldier that made our studio complete.

RABBIT

1939

1940

Bugs, for once full of carrots: LUMBER JACK-RABBIT *(1954)*

ike some embryos and all babies, animated characters can be a burden and an irritation to those who bear them. As in the case of Bugs Bunny, the gestation period may drag on for two or three years before you can even be sure you have a baby, much less see it grow up. A time period that may be pleasant and to be expected in a lady elephant is a source of frustration to an animator.

In Bugs's case, there appeared in a few early cartoons a sort of unfertilized half-cel of creativity, wandering wanly around our films, searching for its better—or bitter—half. A crude creature, half—or perhaps only a quarter—completed, but within it was a tiny spark of creativity.

For me this spark surfaced—although I did not recognize it at the time—in a cartoon film I directed in 1938 called *Prest-o Change-o*, released in March of 1939. In their fine source book *The Warner Brothers Cartoons,** Will Friedwald and Jerry Beck gave this outline of that cartoon:

"Two curious puppies come in from the storm into an old dark house. They soon encounter a bizarrely magical white rabbit, who comes out of a magic hat to lead them on a merry chase, constantly doing tricks to perplex them . . . The rabbit is truly a funny animal."

* *Scarecrow Press, 1981.*

Well, maybe. But it *is* true that the rabbit, to my surprise as well as the dog's, did kiss one of them, an act not to be confused in importance with "Veni, Vidi, Vici," but still, to my knowledge, a rabbit had never kissed a dog before, although I had an aunt who preferred kissing her poodle to kissing me, a source of relief to all concerned.

The development of a major character such as Bugs, Daffy Duck, Porky Pig, etc.—unlike most forms of life—was a hopscotch affair, moving from director to director to director, picking up and dropping comic turns and comedic characteristics of possible use to the mature character. But none of this was deliberate. We not only didn't know that there was a comic genius brewing in our group, we didn't even know we were pregnant. For me, certainly, the idea that any film of mine would contribute any useful trait to an immortal cartoon character like Bugs or Daffy would have carried pretentiousness to absolute absurdity.

Besides *Prest-o Change-o*, our embryonic rabbit went through two other stages before emerging as a highly interesting, surprising, and very funny baby in Tex Avery's *A Wild Hare* in 1940:

1st stage: *Porky's Hare Hunt* (April 1938). The directorial team of Bugs Hardaway and Cal Dalton tried in this film to adopt the existing and unfinished character of Daffy Duck, including "Woo-woos!" into a rabbit skin. But the Daffy they were imitating bore little or no relationship to the wonderfully suave, grasping, greedy, and altogether wonderful superduck of the future. However, to coin a phrase already coined, "gold and surnames are where you find them." Our rabbit found his in the following way. There was in residence at the then Schlesinger Studio a character designer named Charles Thorson, who had designed Little Hiawatha and others at Disney. Hardaway asked him to design a rabbit for *Porky's Hare Hunt*.

Fairly modern rabbit

Thorson did so and sent back the accompanying model sheet, labeled, naturally enough, "Bugs' bunny." Just as he would have labeled it "Chuck's bunny" if it had been for me. The Curies' discovery of uranium fades into insignificance in the light of such a historic moment.

2nd stage: *Elmer's Candid Camera* (March 1940), direction by some happily long-forgotten director named Charles M. Jones. (Leon Schlesinger thought it undignified to use nicknames, so we were respectively—if not respectfully—Charles M. Jones, I. Freleng, Robert McKimson, Robert Clampett, and Fred Avery. Schlesinger also thought the term "director" undignified, so we appeared on all early credits as "supervisors.") In this cartoon we find Bugs stumbling, fumbling, and mumbling around, vainly seeking a personality on which to hang his dia-

Embryonic rabbit—fairly full-fledged Elmer, 1940

196

logue and action, or—in better words than mine—"walking around with his umbilical in his hand, looking for some place to plug it in." It is obvious when one views this cartoon, which I recommend only if you are dying to die of ennui, that my conception of timing and dialogue was formed by watching the action in the La Brea tar pits. It would be complimentary to call it sluggish. Not only Bugs suffered at my hands, but difficult as it is to make an unassertive character like Elmer Fudd into a flat, complete schmuck, I managed.

Perhaps the kindest thing to say about *Elmer's Candid Camera* is that it taught everyone what *not* to do and how not to do it.

Ah-ha! Life begins! A baby finally born and the long gestation period is fully justified in:

A Wild Hare (July 1940), directed by Tex Avery. In this film, through the brilliant, wild, and stimulating mind of Tex Avery, we catch a remarkable first glimpse of the possibilities implicit in the personality of Warner Bros. Cartoons' first true star.

CARRY 3
HAIRS ON BACK
OF SKULL

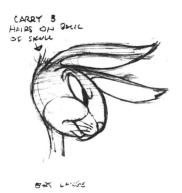

Bugs in transit

You-know-who's coat of arms by C. Jones, that old armorial student

Consider the elements that Tex introduced: the incongruously hilarious classic line "What's up, Doc?" and the sadly hopeful appeal to the audience by Elmer Fudd, "Be vewy, vewy quiet, I'm hunting wabbits!"; Bugs's volatile unpredictability and sudden changes of mood; the quick timing—new to us all—and the utilization of all parts of Bugs's anatomy (his ears as propellers, for instance; his hand coming out of the hole alone, strolling about on two fingers, checking the carrot and Elmer's rifle, making a huge take and diving back into the hole). Actually, Tex was exploring not only two divergent characters but also their symbiotic relationship, their need for each other: Bugs Bunny's agonized theatrical death throes after being "shot" and Elmer's equally remorseful bewailments are a perfect example of this symbiosis.

So Bugs Bunny could now live happily ever after; the perfect example stood before us. All we had to do was follow Tex's lead. The only problem was, none of us knew or could figure out what Tex had done right. Including Tex.

Because, in Tex's second directorial effort with Bugs, in *Tortoise Beats Hare* (March 1941), after a wonderfully funny opening in which Bugs walks out in front of the main title and credits and reads them aloud—"Fray-ud Av-very; Dave Mono-a-han, Char-lus Mack-Himp-sun"—Tex apparently forgot what Bugs was all about, and the tortoise becomes the wisecracking wiseacre, humiliating Bugs at every turn. The tortoise in fact becomes Bugs, and Bugs becomes Elmer Fudd, outwitted and outacted, thereby losing control both of the tortoise-hare race and of the picture itself.

Friz Freleng stepped into the picture in June 1941 with *Hiawatha's Rabbit Hunt*, and he, too, joined Tex and me in not quite understanding what the hell was going on, and he, too, went wide of the mark in understanding Bugs's persona. Not as wide as I did and Tex did, but 'twas enough, 'twould serve.

Fortunately for all of us, Tex was back on track in July 1941 with *The Heckling Hare*. As Jerry Beck and Will Friedwald wrote: "Willoughby (a dog) goes hunting Bugs Bunny in a wonderful cartoon, featuring so many classic gags, sequences, and lines that it would be futile to attempt to list them all here."

Yes. Bugs was well on his way, and he might have retained his early, Harpo Marx–Groucho Marx-like personality if Tex Avery had not left for M-G-M. But in the hopscotch manner described earlier, Bugs was gradually becoming a more complex character. The writers and directors were all beginning to realize that we had the potential of a brilliant and lasting star on our hands, a rambunctious, unbridled, and often balky baby Bugs that needed now to grow, to smooth out; we must find out how to harness that energy without destroying the spirit and how to guide the child without steering it.

A Wild Hare had certainly won all filmic baby contests so far, but he was still a baby, still incomplete. It was up to us to find out, during the painful growth period—babyhood through childhood so nervously recognizable to all parents. We had to find out *who* Bugs was. We already knew *what* he was.

While learning to walk in a way demonstrative of his unique personality,

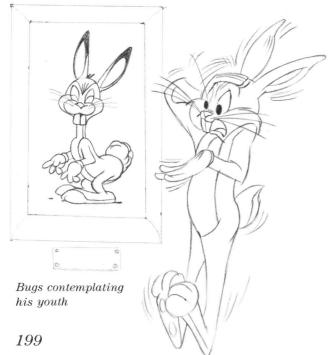

Bugs contemplating his youth

"DRAW POKER.. EH?"

Bugs and Nasty Canasta:
BARBARY COAST BUNNY (1956)

HOW'S THAT.. DO I WIN?

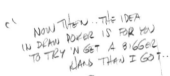

NOW THEN...THE IDEA IN DRAW POKER IS FOR YOU TO TRY 'N GET A BIGGER HAND THAN I GOT..

Bugs went through a period of wild awkwardness before settling into the self-contained studied attitudes peculiar to him, so that his every movement is Bugs and Bugs only, just as his speech developed from a kind of vaudevillian patois loaded with "deses" and "doses" to a fully cadenced speech in which he studiously inserts an occasional "ain't" in the same casual way as an Oxford graduate does.

In short, all fat had to be removed from his dialogue, his figure, and his behavior. We were, in volleying Bugs back and forth from director to director, developing the heart and muscles of a mature and believable character.

I think we all would have been embarrassed if one of us had tried to state what was happening in philosophic or logical terms. Logic and philosophy were certainly there, underlying the growth of our characters. But we were shy of pontification as well as of aesthetic theorizing or critique. Only in retrospect can we see that there was a deep and innocent knowledge forming within this heterogeneous and varied crew, and that knowledge produced the atmosphere for all the other characters who grew to maturity during those same years, between 1941 and 1950, and beyond. During those years we learned what was funny without analyzing *why* it was funny, and, even more important, what was *not* funny.

So Bugs Bunny was in the good hands of parents who loved and admired him, who were good-humored and constantly surprised and pleased by his antics and by those of his playfellows, just as all good and sensible parents are, and who were just as uncertain as parents are about our contributions to the children's growth. Nevertheless, we watched carefully for that flash of individuality, that spark of the unusual, that happy accident that could be encouraged and developed into the interesting, stimulating, and sympathetic adult we would all like our children to become.

"It isn't as though I haven't lived up to my contract...goodneth knows I've done that..."

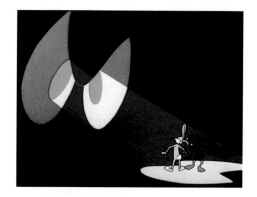

Inside view of Elmer's skull

201 *Art critics art critiquing*

"I beg your pardon, sir, but could you direct me to the shortest route to the Coachella Valley and the Great Carrot Festival... pant! pant!... therein?"

Wile E. Coyote, looking surprisingly like Ken Harris in a Batman suit, heads for glory

Haute couture in RABBIT OF SEVILLE

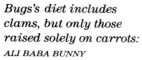

Bugs's diet includes
clams, but only those
raised solely on carrots:
ALI BABA BUNNY

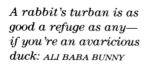

A rabbit's turban is as
good a refuge as any—
if you're an avaricious
duck: *ALI BABA BUNNY*

203

*Daffy (Robin Hood) Duck
demonstrating the efficacy
of a "buck and a quarter"
quarterstaff over and off the rack
to a skeptical Friar Porky*

*Daffy: "And perhaps I, foppish
that I am—might be the Scarlet
Pumpernickel?"*

*Bereft, bothered, and bemildred
(Walt Kelly) Princess finds that
she must marry the dethpicable
Grand Duke*

*One can only suppose that the
exquisite authenticity of this
boudoir scene came from actual
experience by Maurice Noble and
Phil De Guard*

In the twentieth century a singing frog equals $$$$...

...likewise in the twenty-first century

Maurice Noble's arming Elmer was a noble but fruitless gesture in this inspirational sketch for WHAT'S OPERA, DOC?

(NEAR LEFT) The giant shadow in our loving tribute to the majesty of Vladimir Tytla's "Night on Bald Mountain"

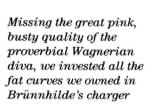

Missing the great pink, busty quality of the proverbial Wagnerian diva, we invested all the fat curves we owned in Brünnhilde's charger

Tatiana Riabouchinska and David Lichine were unwitting contributors to the authenticity of this bit of terpsichore

(LEFT) Probably never in the entire history of cinema has anyone uttered the deathless lines of "I'll kiww the wabbit!" with greater dramatic clarity. The sound you hear is Edwin Booth stirring jealously in his sepulcher

207

*In the background our
entire corps de ballet can
be seen...Oh, we were big
on joie de vivre!
Toujour gai, etc., aussi!*

NUDE DUCK DESCENDING A STAIRCASE

*You have to be a little crazy to
paint like Van Gogh and you
have to be a little crazier to try
to paint like Van Gogh*

Great comedians are *always* sympathetic; Oliver Hardy, Stan Laurel, Jack Benny, Richard Pryor, Robin Williams are *not* stand-up comedians. It is not *what* they say, it is always how they say it that evokes sympathy, laughter, and affection. And each is discrete; we can recognize their individual attitudes and characteristics so well that they can be imitated by having those characteristics copied—the mark of all great comedians.

Great comic lines are seldom funny in themselves, which would be a death knell to the stand-up comedian, because he is tickling your ear, not your heart. Jack Benny's "Well." is hardly a funny line in itself; it is funny in the context of his personality, just as "What's up, Doc?" is not humorous in and of itself. It is very funny in the context of a scene that has been carefully and incongruously structured to make the line an absurdity. One does not, after all, stroll up to a hunter pouring bullets into one's domicile and, after a casual nip at a carrot, just as casually inquire, "What's up, Doc?" Daffy Duck's perfectly logical report to the audience—"Pronoun trouble"—has in the abstract no meaning at all, rational or humorous, without an elaborate and frustrating harangue between Daffy and Bugs Bunny over the ever present Duck Season?/Rabbit Season? dilemma.

Early Elmer and developing Bugs: HARE TONIC *(1945)*

Bugs "Daffy Duck" Bunny

and bewildered Elmer

and Daffy "Bugs Bunny" Duck: RABBIT FIRE *(1951)*

209

In super-rabbit *(1943) I began to get some remote idea of what Bugs Bunny was all about*

Humorous dialogue, we discovered, is not what is said; it is *where* it is said, *how* it is said, *who* is doing the saying, and who are the characters involved and/or physically or verbally responsive to that dialogue. Where would the insane common sense of Groucho be without the beautiful illogic of Chico, or the unpredictable but also logical response of Harpo: "Three cheers for Captain Spaulding" not only becomes "Three chairs for Captain Spaulding"; the chairs appear too. Yes, underlying *all* humor is the necessary logic, believability, and ultimate sympathy that is the touchstone of humor.

But the discovery that these were not philosophic but entirely practical matters led me struggling and squirming down that rabbit hole until I could see the light at the end of the tunnel.

Each of the following films contributed something to my knowledge of Bugs Bunny as I saw and could understand him:

210

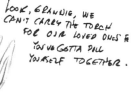

LOOK, GRANNIE, WE CAN'T CARRY THE TORCH FOR OUR LOVED ONES ﬀ YOU'VE GOTTA PULL YOURSELF TOGETHER.

CASE OF THE MISSING HARE (DECEMBER 1942)
SUPER-RABBIT (APRIL 1943)
HARE CONDITIONED (AUGUST 1945)

And when as a director I did burst forth, I found awaiting me a rabbit far different from Tex Avery's wild hare. Why was this necessary? Because I am not Tex Avery. (The Greek chorus moans: "More's the pity.") I could not animate a character I could laugh at but could not understand. A wild wild hare was not for me; what I needed was a character with the spicy, somewhat erudite introspection of a Professor Higgins, who, when nettled or threatened, would respond with the swagger of D'Artagnan as played by Errol Flynn, with the articulate quick-wittedness of Dorothy Parker—in other words, the Rabbit of My Dreams.

This Bugs Bunny is far too strong a character to behave as an early Daffy Duck or a late Woody Woodpecker acts. It is no part of his character to go out and bedevil anyone for mischief's sake alone.

Golden Rule. Bugs must always be provoked. In every film, someone must have designs upon his person: gastronomic, as a trophy, as a good-luck piece (rabbit's foot, which makes as

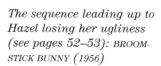

The sequence leading up to Hazel losing her ugliness (see pages 52–53): BROOM-STICK BUNNY (1956)

PUSH HA (SWORD) ANHD.

SPROING!!

much sense as a rabbit carrying a human foot on a key chain), as an unwilling participant in a scientific experiment (laboratory rabbit or outer-space creature). Without such threats, Bugs is far too capable a rabbit to evoke the necessary sympathy.

From *Hair-Raising Hare* (May 1946) on, I did not have to ask for whom the rabbit toiled; he toiled for me. I no longer drew pictures of Bugs; I drew Bugs, I timed Bugs, I *knew* Bugs, because what Bugs aspired to, I too aspired to. Aside from a few stumbles, Bugs and I were always at ease with one another.

Lobby card sketch for DUCK! RABBIT! DUCK! *(1953)*

In response to a constantly repeated question, my constantly repeated response is: No, I do not have a favorite character, Bugs or anyone else. Bugs Bunny and Pepé Le Pew are concordant with my aspirations; Daffy Duck, Wile E. Coyote, Elmer Fudd, to mention a few of the losers in our stable, constitute rueful recognition, but every character has contributed to my own development as a writer-director-animator. I also have but few favorite pictures, but I do remember what I call "corner" pictures—those that, as in turning a corner in a strange city, reveal new and enchanting vistas. Among these films, some of which involved Bugs Bunny:

Haredevil Hare (July 1948). The first of our outer-space cartoons, and the first appearance of Marvin Martian and his Illudium Q-36 Space Modulator.

Long-Haired Hare (June 1949). The first of a series of films in which music was the dictating factor.

Frigid Hare (October 1949). This may have been the first time Bugs missed that "left turn at Albuquerque" and also in which he is a rescuer (of a baby penguin) and not a victim.

Rabbit of Seville (December 1950). This was, for me, the first cartoon in which the music absolutely determined the action.

Rabbit Fire (May 1951). The first of the Duck Season/Rabbit Season collisions with Daffy Duck. A final touch I always liked was that it turned out to be Elmer Season.

Bully for Bugs (August 1953). In the classic confrontation with an outsized rival, this was perhaps the most satisfying structurally. The bull was certainly a worthy opponent to Bugs. And equally satisfactory was the fact that I was ordered by Eddie Selzer not to make any pictures about bullfights. "Bullfights aren't funny!" he said. Since he had never been right in any edict up to that time, it was obvious there was something very funny in the bullring.

Hänsel? Hänsel?

Puzzled Prince:
BEWITCHED BUNNY (1954)

Bewitched Bunny (July 1954) and Beanstalk Bunny (February 1955). Getting Bugs and later Daffy mixed in with Hansel and Gretel and a witch whose hobby was eating children, and Elmer Fudd as the Giant at the top of the beanstalk, was too much to resist.

Ali Baba Bunny (February 1957). Just weak, I guess, but I could not possibly miss seeing Bugs and Daffy get involved with the giant Hassan ("Hassan chop!") and the Genie of the Lamp.

What's Opera, Doc? (July 1957). For sheer production quality, magnificent music, and wonderful animation, this is probably our most elaborate and satisfying production.

Those Bugs features were the most important to me of our corner films, although some of the last cartoons we did at Warner Bros.—Hare Way to the Stars (March 1958), Baton Bunny (January 1959), Rabbit's Feat (June 1960) with Wile E. Coyote, and The Abominable Snow Rabbit (May 1961)—I think continued to show a fully rounded, intelligent, and funny rabbit.

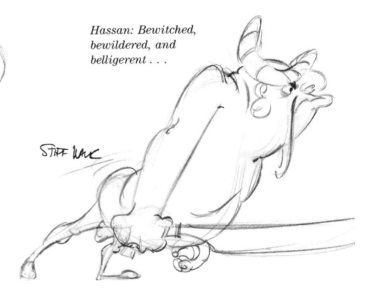

Hassan: Bewitched, bewildered, and belligerent . . .

STIFF WALK

214

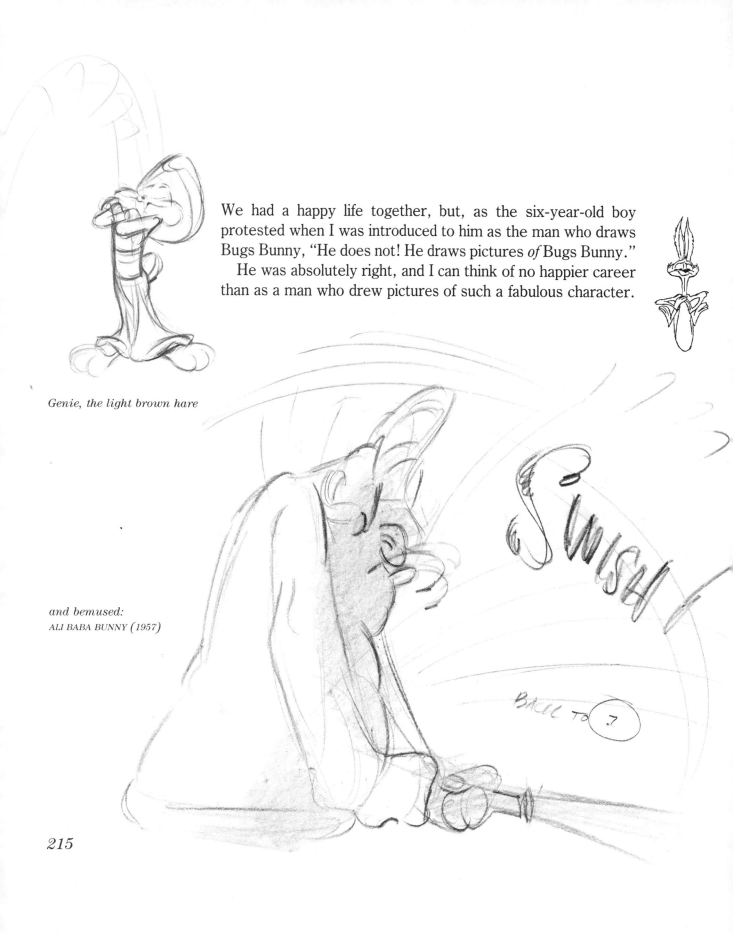

We had a happy life together, but, as the six-year-old boy protested when I was introduced to him as the man who draws Bugs Bunny, "He does not! He draws pictures *of* Bugs Bunny."

He was absolutely right, and I can think of no happier career than as a man who drew pictures of such a fabulous character.

Genie, the light brown hare

and bemused:
ALI BABA BUNNY (1957)

SWISH!

BACK TO .7

215

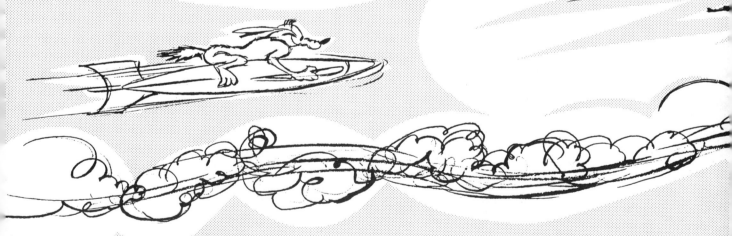

NEVER
TAKE A RIGHT
TURN AT
ALBUQUERQUE

BEEP-
BEEP!

I suppose it would be nice if I knew the age and social structure of my audience, but the truth is, I make cartoons for me. This wasn't always true. In my more intellectual youth I tried studying audiences—making notes and timing laughs and applause. And the more I learned about audiences, the worse my cartoons grew. So I gave it up and concentrated on learning a little bit about everything that interested me and a lot about drawing, until my hand would respond to what my mind dictated and my brain became a treasure house of pertinent trivia. Then, oddly enough, my cartoons began to evoke laughter.

In the Road Runner cartoons, we hoped to evoke sympathy for the Coyote. It is the basis of the series: the Coyote tries by any means to capture the Road Runner, ostensibly and at first to eat him, but this motive has become beclouded, and it has become, in my mind at least, a question of loss of dignity that forces him to continue. And who is the Coyote's enemy? Why, the Coyote. The Road Runner has never touched him, never even startled him intentionally beyond coming up behind the Coyote occasionally and going "Beep-Beep!"

No, the only enemy the Coyote has is his overwhelming stubbornness. Like all of us, at least some of the time, he persists in a course of action long after he has forgotten his original reasons for embarking on it.

The Coyote is a history of my own frustration and war with all tools, multiplied only slightly. I can remember that my wife and daughter would start to weep bitterly and seek hiding places

C.J. at home, Tareco Drive, Hollywood, about 1960

219

whenever they saw me head toward the tool drawer, if only to hang a picture. I have never reached into that devilish drawer without starting a chain of errors and disasters of various but inevitable proportions. Like any other man, I would rather succeed in what I can't do than do what I have successfully done before. I have never reached into that drawer without encountering one of those spiny things you stick flowers in. We don't keep that thing in that drawer, but it is always there. I count it a good day when I get only one spine under a fingernail. I tried to get the spiny thing out of the drawer once, but found out that the last time, when it had stuck to four fingers at once and been in fact lifted a few inches out of its nest in the resulting shriek, it had fallen on a tube of glue, puncturing the tube and affixing itself to the drawer for all time. I have tried lackadaisically from time to time to remove it, and have succeeded in

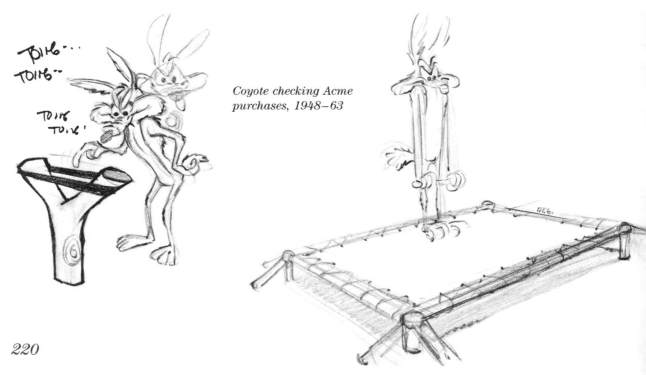

Coyote checking Acme
purchases, 1948–63

220

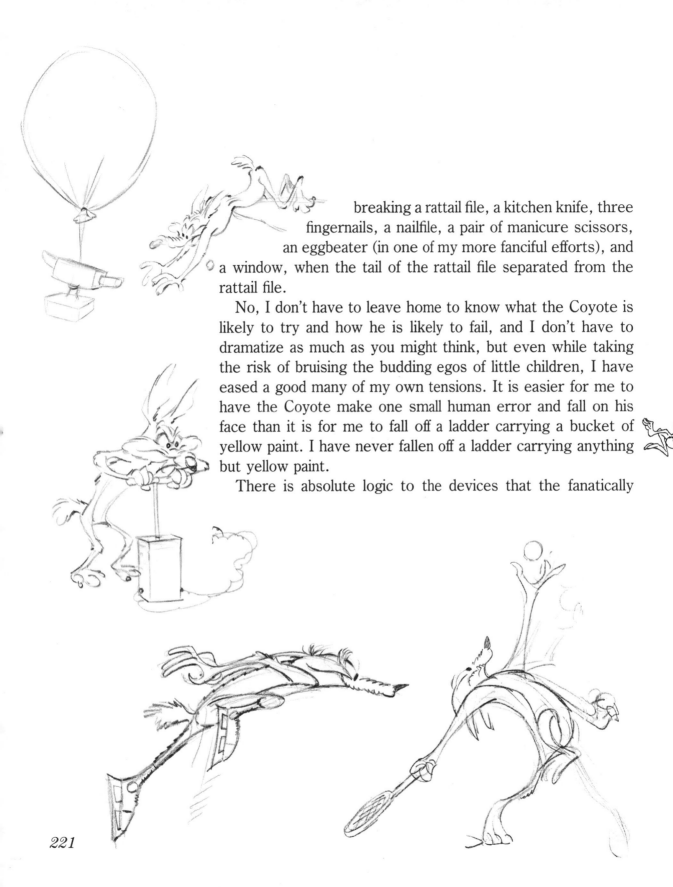

breaking a rattail file, a kitchen knife, three fingernails, a nailfile, a pair of manicure scissors, an eggbeater (in one of my more fanciful efforts), and a window, when the tail of the rattail file separated from the rattail file.

No, I don't have to leave home to know what the Coyote is likely to try and how he is likely to fail, and I don't have to dramatize as much as you might think, but even while taking the risk of bruising the budding egos of little children, I have eased a good many of my own tensions. It is easier for me to have the Coyote make one small human error and fall on his face than it is for me to fall off a ladder carrying a bucket of yellow paint. I have never fallen off a ladder carrying anything but yellow paint.

There is absolute logic to the devices that the fanatically

. . . and more products

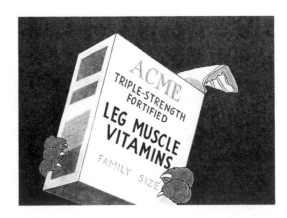

single-minded Coyote uses. They *should* work, but there's always one tiny thing wrong, and, as with most of us, that tiny thing leads to disaster. Human beings, of course, in even their most grandiloquent plans, often resemble coyotes. Instance: in one of our government's first efforts at space exploitation, the element that failed in that half-billion-dollar unmanned space rocket cost thirty-five cents. It seems obvious that the government was poaching on the Coyote's territory. That thirty-five-cent article was obviously purchased from the Acme Corporation.

The Acme Corporation stemmed from games the Jones tads played in their juvenile dotage. My sister Dorothy fell in love with the title Acme, finding that it was adopted by many struggling and embryonic companies because it put them close to the top of their chosen services in the Yellow Pages. Today, of course, it is commonplace to see AAAAA Cleaners and Dyers or AAABBBCCCDDD Drugs, which sounds like a Porky Pig establishment. But in those simple days such verbal chicanery was unheard of—Acme was a word; it was that simple.

So, many years later, it seemed logical to use Acme in our films, from Acme Dancing Academy for Infant Ducks to the Acme Corporation we put on our door when Chuck Jones, Inc., lived on the twelfth floor at Sunset and Vine, followed by our slogan: *"We build fine Acmes."*

(CARNIVERUS VULGARIS)

First models of Road Runner and Coyote

Long before that, however, the Acme Corporation had become the sole supplier to Wile E. Coyote. Whatever his needs were, the Acme Corporation was there to supply. It was a perfect symbiotic relationship; no money was ever involved. The Acme Corporation supplied the Coyote's requirements: Acme Jet-Propelled Roller Skates, Acme Burmese Tiger Trap, Acme Leg Muscle Vitamins, Acme Female Road Runner Costume, Acme Batman Outfit, etc. All of them *almost* perfect. But surely the jet-propulsion group should have eschewed the use of the Acme Little Giant Bobrick, even at the bargain rate of thirty-five cents.

The rules and disciplines are properly difficult to identify. But there are—there must be—rules. Without them, comedy slops over at the edges. Identity is lost. "Comedy is not so much what you do," said Groucho Marx, "as what you don't do." The rules that apply to Chico or to Harpo do not apply to Groucho. Groucho stands between Chico, who speaks with charming illogic, and Harpo, who acts with equally charming physical illogic. Groucho, in his own way, balances them with his own version of logic. Being led by Chico into a strange fourth-dimensional argument about purchasing and/or building a house, he says, "No. It will have to be over here. I don't want Junior crossing the railroad tracks on his way to reform school."

Only Groucho could say that line. He is always well within his self-made rules. And they become logical only because he demands that they be obeyed.

During Laurel and Hardy's long feud with Edgar Kennedy and Jimmy Finlayson, the most astonishing discipline was one that contradicted all existing rules of combat; namely, you can't do anything to me when I'm doing something to you. In one of their early encounters with Kennedy, he methodically destroyed their car while they were destroying his house in the Christmas-tree salesman episode. Taking turns, each would rip off a fender, break a window, smash a headlight, or rip up a tree, *without* interference from his opponent. These were fights in which there was no defense, only offense. A strange and unique rule—but one of the most hilarious in the annals of comedy.

Just as I later decided that there would be no dialogue in the Coyote–Road Runner series because it seemed like a good rule, or indeed it would become a good rule if it was consistent; *all* comedians obey rules consistent with their own view of comedy. In my opinion, Jackie Gleason got more mileage out of threatening to hit somebody than the Three Stooges ever did by doing so.

Here were some of the rules we obeyed in the Coyote–Road Runner series:

RULE 1. THE ROAD RUNNER CANNOT HARM THE COYOTE EXCEPT BY GOING "BEEP-BEEP!"

RULE 2. NO OUTSIDE FORCE CAN HARM THE COYOTE—ONLY HIS OWN INEPTITUDE OR THE FAILURE OF THE ACME PRODUCTS.

RULE 3. THE COYOTE COULD STOP ANYTIME—*IF* HE WERE NOT A FANATIC. (REPEAT: "A FANATIC IS ONE WHO REDOUBLES HIS EFFORT WHEN HE HAS FORGOTTEN HIS AIM."—GEORGE SANTAYANA)

RULE 4. NO DIALOGUE EVER, EXCEPT "BEEP-BEEP!"

RULE 5. THE ROAD RUNNER MUST STAY ON THE ROAD—OTHERWISE, LOGICALLY, HE WOULD NOT BE CALLED ROAD RUNNER.

RULE 6. ALL ACTION MUST BE CONFINED TO THE NATURAL ENVIRONMENT OF THE TWO CHARACTERS—THE SOUTHWEST AMERICAN DESERT.

RULE 7. ALL MATERIALS, TOOLS, WEAPONS, OR MECHANICAL CONVENIENCES MUST BE OBTAINED FROM THE ACME CORPORATION.

RULE 8. WHENEVER POSSIBLE, MAKE GRAVITY THE COYOTE'S GREATEST ENEMY.

RULE 9. THE COYOTE IS ALWAYS MORE HUMILIATED THAN HARMED BY HIS FAILURES.

The above are pertinent illustrations of the kind of thinking that went into the making of these films.

The Road Runner and Coyote cartoons are known and accepted throughout the world—perhaps the lack of dialogue is one reason. If you want to laugh, you can do so at any time, whether in Danish, French, Japanese, Urdu, Navajo, Eskimo, Portuguese, or Hindi. "Beep-Beep!" is the Esperanto of comedy.

I don't suppose the Coyote ever actually left chocolaty paw prints on old Sears, Roebuck catalogues on the desert, but many years later Mike Maltese and I at least were able to supply him with the Acme catalogue.

While the Coyote had lurked somewhere in the cluttered back rooms of my mind ever since, at the age of seven, I read about this enchanting creature in Mark Twain's *Roughing It*— just waiting for a chance to star—it wasn't until I was more than grown that the opportunity came up. It was 1947 and the American animated short subject was preoccupied with the chase. Everyone seemed to be engaged in the pursuit of one another: Tom after Jerry; Elmer Fudd and Yosemite Sam after Bugs Bunny; Porky Pig after Daffy Duck; Bluto and Popeye having it out. So, as all writers and directors must have, Mike and I felt the call of Profundity. We would do a satire on chases, show up the shallowness of the whole concept, and become the Dean Swifts or H. L. Menckens of our day, be honored by learned societies, and probably welcomed at unemployment agencies nationwide.

The first Road Runner and Coyote cartoon, *Fast and Furryous*, was an absolute and dismal failure, as satire. And it was wholly and unexpectedly and undeservedly a success, as comedy. Robert Benchley said of *Abie's Irish Rose*: "The public not only took the play to its bosom, it rubbed its bosom to a nubbin hugging it."

"If you cannot lick 'em, join 'em." A nice aphorism for the embarrassed parodist, so we gracefully accepted the kudos as

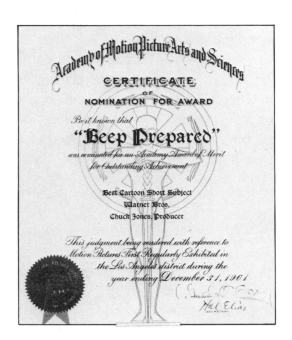

*Academy Award
Nomination, 1961*

though this had been our intent all the time, and lived happily with the Coyote and Road Runner ever after.

In animated cartoons, we do generally prefer animals to humans. First, if your story calls for human beings, use live action. It is cheaper, quicker, and more believable. If, as a director, I could train a live coyote and a live road runner to act, I would use them. I am an animator and an animation director; therefore, I look for characters that *cannot* be done in live action. That is what animation is all about; it is an extension beyond the ability of live-action motion pictures. Second, as said, it is easier to humanize animals than it is to humanize humans. We are far too close to other human beings; we are surrounded by human beings; we are subconsciously and consciously critical of other human beings according to how they deviate from our own behavior or from standards of behavior we approve of. Therefore, to many of us, everyone who looks like a cokehead *is* a cokehead. Everyone who looks like a bum *is* a bum. But, if so, what about the talent of Theodore Dreiser, who looked like an unmade bed? If all wimpy-looking people *are* wimps, what about Woody Allen?

It is in order to avoid these stereotypes that animators, as well as Aesop, Kipling, La Fontaine, E. B. White, Beatrix Potter, Felix Salten, Walt Kelly, and countless other writers, turn to animals. People look at rabbits or ducks or bears as a class rather than as individuals, though it is true we stereotype those classes. We classify all snakes as repulsive or dangerous, when fewer than one snake in a million can or will harm us. We are revolted by spiders, when most spiders are beneficial to mankind and only one spider in a million is harmful to man,

227

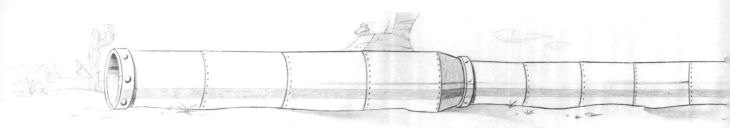

and then, like the snake, only if provoked.

Working against those stereotypes, animation directors and writers have attempted to explode human prejudices: E. B. White's heroine in *Charlotte's Web* was a spider; one of Rudyard Kipling's heroes in *The Jungle Book* was a thirty-foot python who loved a small boy, not as an hors d'oeuvre but as a friend. Bugs Bunny grew into a comic hero with the kind of

"DAWG"

*From Bob McKimson's
Foghorn Leghorn series*

Mysterious pipe: SOUP OR SONIC, *episode from* BUGS BUNNY'S BUSTIN' OUT ALL OVER (CBS-TV, 1980)

human characteristics we admire and laugh with, because no one would expect a rabbit to have any personality at all. After all, rabbits are rabbits, aren't they? Just as with Daffy Duck, a wimpy duck with the ego of a Stallone—come now, ducks quack, that's about it with ducks. How about Pepé Le Pew? A skunk with an overwhelming confidence in his own desirability?

Everyone knows what a pussycat most pussycats are, yet Sylvester Cat is a poltroon, a fanatic, a graceless boor, cunning in an awkward way and a terrible singer; in short, Sylvester is very much like I am, only a little more so.

I have long felt that dogs—unlike cats—are professionals, and Charlie Dog is just a sterling example of that professionalism. A cat is a cat. Period. From the time that the cat first condescended to let man and woman feed, scratch, and pet him, with no obligation on his part to do anything in return, the cat has resisted almost every effort to change his appearance, his size, or his temperament for the convenience of man. He insists on walking on his wild lone. Whereas the dog, who started out as stalwart, strong, wild, and wolf-like, has flopped over on his kowtowable back, legs astraddle, and allowed man to convert him into everything from a Mexican hairless to a great Dane (usually with weak hindquarters), from the smashed-in nose of the pug and the English bull to the pointy nose of the Russian wolfhound and the collie. Yes, man put on his genetic gloves and pummeled, smashed, pulled, tugged noble dog into shapes so remote from the original that a chihuahua could mate with a Saint Bernard only with the help of a stepladder and a midwife, and all this with the active and apparently enthusiastic assistance of the dog.

Contrast this with the "domestic" cat. The same energy poured forth by man to reform the dog has had only the following results with the cat: We have varied the length and color of the cat's hair. We have observed and tried to take credit for the tailless Manx cat, the Siamese cat, and other variations. But there is no scientific evidence but that the cat arranged these variations for its own convenience. Try as we may, we have been unable to vary the size and weight of cats as contrasted with dogs: one (1) Labrador retriever equals twenty-five (25) Yorkies. The cat stubbornly (and serenely) sticks to its own proper range of size and weight. The smallest and the largest domestic cats vary in almost exactly the same ratio as

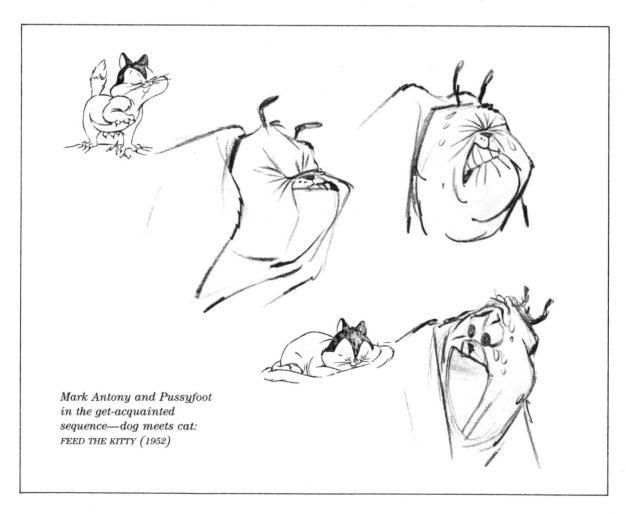

Mark Antony and Pussyfoot
in the get-acquainted
sequence—dog meets cat:
FEED THE KITTY (1952)

Sam Sheepdog going to well-merited rest: A SHEEP IN THE DEEP *(1962)*

do human beings, excluding nature's genetic eccentricities: midgets and giants. Human beings range normally from perhaps 4′10″ to 6′4″ and from 100 to 220 pounds. Twenty percent variation in height to around fifty percent in weight, and so it is with cats.

A cat is a cat is a cat. And that is it.

A dog can be a lapdog; a watchdog; a fawning, servile slob; a violent, murderous bastard; a kissy, big-hearted, great-eyed, crawly lover—and is really and too often an abysmal caricature of the worst in mankind. You feed him, cuff him, pull his ears, slap him silly, it's all one to him. "I knew he was my master," says the Kid in Richard Harding Davis's *The Bar Sinister*, "because he kicked me."

If you make a fool of yourself in front of a cat, he will sneer at you, if you are sober; he will leave the room if you are drunk. If you make a fool of yourself in front of a dog, he will make a fool of himself, too.

Charlie is the first honest dog I ever met. He freely admits that he is out to get adopted and will use *any* method available to achieve his purpose. He may not be lovable, but he most certainly is honest. "You ain't got no pet, I ain't got no master," he points out to the owner of a posh restaurant in *A Hound for Trouble*. "I'll make you a preposition." In *Dog Gone South*, in an effort to impress a Southern plantation owner, he assumed the identity of a Rebel soldier returning from Gettysburg: "Oh, suh, it was horrible, Yankees to the left, Yankees to the right, but ah saved the regiment." He dies saluting and sobbing, "Chitlins forever!"

So, just as Bugs is not your ordinary rabbit, Charlie is not your ordinary dog. Bugs, as a rabbit, is uniquely notable for intrepidity and love of combat; Charlie, as a dog, is remarkable for honesty.

The Birth in Me of a Daffy Duckling

THIS LOOKS LIKE A JOB FOR...

I have watched with fascination his [Daffy's] growth from his earliest haphazard puerile personality, through adolescence, to the splendid bombast of his maturity in the fifties. Daffy has become the spokesman for the egoist in everyone, but he remains always undaunted by the inevitable requital: the fear of consequences that makes cowards of the rest of us.

— **ROBERT D. TSCHIRGI, M.D., PH.D.**
Professor of Neurosciences
University of California, La Jolla
February 14, 1985

DRIPALONG DAFFY (1951)

THE MASKED AVENGER—RIGHTER OF WRONGS! DOER OF HEROIC DEEDS— RIDES AGAIN!!

The first surfacing of that part of my character that was later to show up in Daffy Duck occurred at the age of six. My sixth-birthday party, to be precise. I was immensely proud—it seems to me that all my life I have taken the most pride in things over which I have little or no control. Even though I had older sisters, it never occurred to me that anyone had ever become six years old before, and the splendid cake, candles bravely ablaze in salute to my maturity, was ample evidence that I had entered into manhood.

Having blown out the candles and, as a side benefit, managing to send most of the smoke up my little brother's nostrils, I was handed the knife, my first baton of any kind of authority in six misspent years, and was told to cut as large a piece as I liked. At this point Daffy Duck must have had, for me, his earliest beginnings, because I found to my surprise and pleasure that I had no desire to share my cake with anyone. I courteously returned the knife to my mother. I had no need for it, I explained; I would simplify the whole matter by taking the entire cake for myself. Not knowing she had an incipient duck on her hands, she laughed gently and tried to return the knife to my reluctant grasp. I again explained that the knife was superfluous. It was impossible, I pointed out with incontrovertible logic, to cut a cake and still leave it entire for its rightful owner. I had no need and no desire to share.

234

HI-HO TINFOIL !! AWAY-Y-Y-Y-Y!

My father thereupon mounted the hustings (he was nine feet tall and looked like a moose without antlers) and escorted me to my room to contemplate in cakeless solitude the meaning of a word new to me: "selfish." To me then, and to Daffy Duck now, "selfish" means "honest but antisocial"; "unselfish" means "socially acceptable but often dishonest." We all *want* the whole cake, but, unlike Daffy and at least one six-year-old boy, the coward in the rest of us keeps the Daffy Duck, the small boy in us, under control.

"You may cut as large a piece as you want" is a dangerous euphemism. There is a prescribed wedge on every birthday cake that is completely and exactly surrounded by corporal punishment. Exceeding these limits by even a thousandth of an inch brands one as "selfish." From my seventh birthday on, I learned to approach with judgment sharper than a razor's edge this line, without cutting the "un" from "unselfish" to "selfish." I learned very little about social morality but a great deal about survival, and this, after all, is what Daffy Duck is all about.

"Of all the characters you have worked with, do you have a favorite?"

I've been told that long lists tend to cause readers' eyes to glaze over, but the astonishing number of characters I have worked with must be inserted somewhere. It might as well be here.

Consider (and these are not all, by any means):

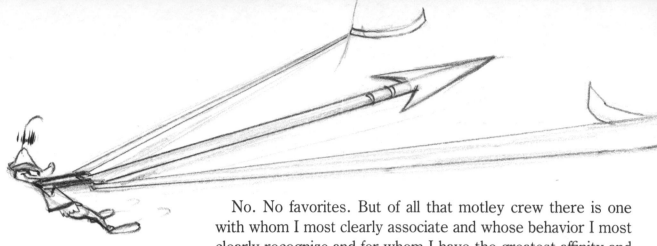
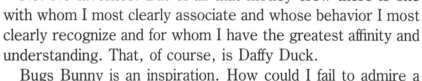

Final try: ROBIN HOOD DAFFY
(1958)

Deducting Aunt Mehitabel's
expenses: DEDUCE, YOU SAY
(1956)

No. No favorites. But of all that motley crew there is one with whom I most clearly associate and whose behavior I most clearly recognize and for whom I have the greatest affinity and understanding. That, of course, is Daffy Duck.

Bugs Bunny is an inspiration. How could I fail to admire a character who is equal parts Rex Harrison, D'Artagnan, and Dorothy Parker, packed into a graceful rabbit skin? Daffy is recognition, as is the Coyote.

To quote Richard Thompson (*Film Comment*, January–February 1975): "How do Bugs and Daffy differ? Bugs is a winner and Daffy is a loser" (just like Chaplin, Keaton, Laurel and Hardy, Richard Pryor, and Woody Allen, C.J.). "In these films [*Rabbit Fire*; *Duck! Rabbit! Duck!*; *Rabbit Seasoning*] we have the clearest definition of general roles: Elmer never knows what's going on; Bugs always knows what's going on and is in control of events; Daffy is bright enough to understand how to be in control, but he never quite makes it. Both Bugs and Daffy are talkers, but Daffy talks too much—Daffy's vanity is disastrous. Bugs stands back from a situation, analyzes it, and

"That is a rabbit!": RABBIT
SEASONING *(1952)*

238 DAN

I'M A DIRTY SKUNK?!!

I'M A DIRTY SKUNK!!

DUCK! RABBIT! DUCK! (1953)

makes his move; Daffy becomes emotionally involved, loses his distance, and blows it. He's stuck with a one-track mind which fixes on only one facet of the problem and loses sight of the larger pattern. Bugs is a strong, more traditional American hero—Daffy is much more complicated. He's a coward, he claims, but a live coward—he feels a preemptive necessity to set someone else (Bugs) up for the destruction he knows is stalking him."

In other words, ask not for whom the bell tolls; if I can help it, it tolls for thee.

How am I like Daffy Duck? Let me count the ways:

- Daffy rushes in and fears to tread at the same time.
- "Cowardice," says Daffy, "is its own reward."
- D. Duck Motto: "Shoot a rabbit; save a duck."
- "Ducks are an endangered species; especially me."
- "It is far better to be dethpicable than to be dead."
- "Honesty is the best policy—when everything else fails."
- "I'm different from other people, pain hurts me."
- "If you can't get a half-loaf, take a whole loaf; a whole loaf is better than nothing."

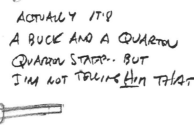

ACTUALLY IT'S A BUCK AND A QUARTER QUARTER STAFF.. BUT I'M NOT TELLING HIM THAT

"AH-HA !!!"

239

ROBIN HOOD DAFFY (1958)

ALI BABA BUNNY (1957)

To sum up: Daffy gallantly and publicly represents all the character traits that the rest of us try to keep subdued. A social amenity to Daffy Duck is simply an unfair block to his desires. To desire, in Daffy's rationale, is to need—as it was to me at six; to need is to acquire, and acquisition is the essence of living. To achieve his ends, he cheerfully and always rationally chews up moral codes by the yard. His rationality may, however, do him in, as in *Rabbit Seasoning*:

BUGS: (To Elmer) Do you want to shoot him now or wait till you get home.

DAFFY: (Protesting) He doesn't have to shoot me now! (To Elmer) Wait till you get home.

ELMER: All wight.

Off arm-in-arm they go to the distant cabin, the door closes; hesitate; the cabin windows light up to the sound of a distant gunshot; hesitate; the cabin door opens to the sound of trap drums; a battered Daffy trudges into the foreground, up to Bugs, grasps him firmly by the neck fur, glares at the undisturbed Bugs.

DAFFY: You're dethpicable!!

Daffy is just like all of us, only more so. Perhaps that's why we find him so appealing.

MY LITTLE DUCKAROO (1954)

DEDUCE, YOU SAY (1956)

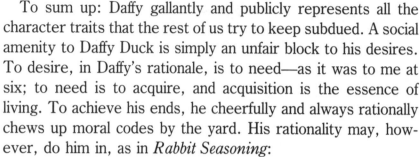

240

Unused dialogue—Daffy
conversing with "J.L."
(Warner): THE SCARLET
PUMPERNICKEL (1950)

EWEPHANT GUN?!

"For shame, Doc, shooting a rabbit with an elephant gun": RABBIT FIRE (1951)

Every great comedian makes himself available to his audience. That is, the traits that define his personality the audience must be able to recognize in themselves—even though, as in the case of Daffy or Bugs, they do not have the courage to exercise them.

I think Daffy wins our admiration for his courage—a courage we probably lack—but we take pride in our wisdom in not pushing in where Daffy fails. We know we are wiser than Daffy, and we can laugh at his foolish failures, but lurking beneath this recognition is a sneaking admiration for his courage.

I know of no great lasting comedian who was not a loser. I know of no beloved comedian *or* actor who was not a loser or a misfit.

The list is both endless and consistent:

Chaplin, Keaton, Lloyd, Ed Wynn, Laurel and Hardy, Abbott and Costello, Donald Duck, Daffy Duck, Wile E. Coyote, Woody Allen, Richard Pryor, Robin Williams.

Why are they so enduring, so endearing? Because they are so much like what we suspect we are, so much like what we are afraid we are.

Most important, I think, they are frail—sometimes heroically frail. Like all the rest of us, they are more recognizable by their mistakes than by their triumphs.

242

BANG!

BANG!

ZINGGG

Even James Bond is one of the world's greatest screwups, to put it mildly, of this or any other century. With every advantage that modern technology can provide, he manages to stumble over the same rake handle we do, only he falls into a swimming pool of piranhas, while we flap into a cow flop.

Fortunately for 007, however, his enemies are just as hamfisted as he is. On one filmic occasion they attempted to spoil his sleep with an attack by a poisonous spider, a simple enough task, one might say—just push a black widow spider through a keyhole—but no, these KGBirds employed a muscular tarantula the size of a cat, a sort of Arnold Schwarzenegger with fur. This gargantuan joker lumbering over the bed awakens even James Bond. The result? A mano-a-mano bit of arm wrestling which the tarantula would have easily won—if it hadn't tripped over five of its unoccupied legs.

James Bond and Daffy Duck—the only difference is that Daffy fails to succeed, while Bond ultimately succeeds in spite of two hours of unmitigated, illogical failures.

"Don't you even know a rabbit when you see one?":
RABBIT FIRE (1951)

SAY . . WHAT'S THE MATTER WITH YOU ANYWAY ?:)

243

Teddy, 1920

TEDDY AND CHARLIE

I always thought
a dog-lover was
a dog who loved
another dog.

— JAMES THURBER

Charlie and Porky:
OFTEN AN ORPHAN (1949)

When I was seven years old, my brother actually hit me with a pie. He didn't mean to. But I had aggravated him and it was the only weapon at hand. He didn't remove the tin plate either, which flattened my face to the point where I could glance into my own ears without discomfort.

The odd thing was that nobody in the family thought it funny at the time, and Mother still thought of it as a waste to the day

245

she died, and set it in her memory as "the time Charles spoiled Sunday dinner for the preacher." The preacher was a pure figment of her imagination, since no preacher could safely enter our house on Sunday. Father said Sunday was a day of rest; six days of religion was enough, and he intended to rest on the seventh, according to the Scriptures. My sister remembers the incident as involving our dog Teddy. She contends I threw Teddy at my brother, who retaliated with the pie. This is obviously untrue. Teddy was a retriever and weighed at least two stone; I could lift him, but I couldn't throw him. For one thing, he was the kind of dog that melts in the middle when you lift him. No matter how high you raised his stomach, his four feet still rested on the ground, and so usually did his ears and, in hot weather, his tongue. No one can throw such a dog . . . it's like throwing a gunnysack full of wet liver.

My point in relating this incident is that humor is a mishap, considered in the proper light. In the past you can be funny even though you are the principal. In the present, mishaps are always funnier if they happen to someone else.

Mike Maltese and I had been playing with the idea of a dog who is the absolute antithesis of all the Noble Hound and Friend of Man persuasion. Charlie was a sort of horizontal Daffy Duck

Teddy contemplating the Pacific Ocean

Teddy at peace

246

with one purpose in life: to be adopted into a cushy, never-more-to-roam pied-à-terre. To be petted, scratched, fed, and spoiled forevermore. Not a bad ambition, and Charlie's failure to accomplish his purpose in his meeting with Farmer Porky Pig is in no wise due to lack of enthusiasm, bravado, over-whelming egotism, or deep lack of the comfort and ease of mind of others, particularly agrarian pigs, as follows:

OFTEN AN ORPHAN   1949

(A Looney Tune)

Charlie trots confidently up to Porky, preoccupied with his farm chores.

CHARLIE: Look, chum, you ain't got no pet, I ain't got no master. (Looks around patronizingly) What a pity, such a lovely farm and no dog. (Taps Porky on chest in a confidential manner) I tell you what I'll do. (Very brightly) I'll make you a preposition: you can be my master and I'll be your dog.

PORKY: (Glances at audience, à la Edgar Kennedy) *No!* N-n-no! I don't want a dog, I don't n-need a—d . . .

CHARLIE: (Strikes elegant pose, taps his own chest, continues inexorably) *I* am fifty percent pointer. (He points in all directions) There it is! There it is! There it is! (Into fighting stance) Fifty percent boxer. (Hits nose with thumb, strutting around an imaginary ring, sniffing and sparring) Fifty percent Irish setter. (Jams clay pipe into mouth, bowl down) Fifty percent watchdog. (Pulls out a pocket watch, checks it carefully) At the tone the time will be—but mostly I'm all labrador receiver!

PORKY: (Disgustedly) Oh—you a-are *not* a labrador receiver!

CHARLIE: (Crestfallen, hurt) I—I'm not?

PORKY: (Angrily) No! You are n-not n-ne-neither no l-labra-d-d-dor retriever!!

CHARLIE: (Blinks, wipes brow, then very reasonably) Look, if you doubt my word, get a labrador and I'll retrieve it for you—that's fair, isn't it?

PORKY: (Somewhat confused and getting more so) A-a-ah-uh-a labra-d-dor . . . Why, uh, sure . . . I-I . . . Ya-you-huh . . .

CHARLIE: (Very quietly) Have you got a labrador?

PORKY: (Scraping foot, embarrassed) N-no.

CHARLIE: Know where you can get a labrador?

PORKY: (Not knowing why, but on the defensive) N-no.

CHARLIE: (Quietly venomous, like George Raft) Then shad-dap.

PORKY: (Begins to boil—rumbling sound of earthquake, kettledrums, steam blows his top) *Get out! Out! Out! Out! Get out!! Out!! Get!! Out!!* (Subsides into hysterical panting)

CHARLIE: (Falls back cringing, looks up piteously at Porky) Y-you mean?

PORKY: *Yes! I mean! Out! Out!! Out!! Ge-get out!!* (Hysterical panting)

CHARLIE: (Hesitantly) Bu-but I thought . . . (Breaks down and cries. Falling to the ground and burying his face in his arms, weeps piteously)

PORKY: (Uncertain softening) Well—gee—you dirty forlorn old dog—I d-didn . . .

CHARLIE: (Blinking and sniffing, talking mainly to blade of

grass he picks up) All my life I've dreamed of the day I could go and live in the country—I'm not strong—I need lotsa fresh air—and milk—and cream. (Tiny cough) And fresh leafy vega-tabbles. (Breaks down and sobs through next sentence) Good clean wholesome farm living. (Cries softly)

PORKY: But I-I—didn't—f . . .

CHARLIE: (Turning sadly away again, ignoring Porky) And now . . . (Big sniff) And now that I've got a chance to regain my health, you want to send me back to the city. (Leaps up stiffly, grabs throat, eyes bulging) *The city!!* I can see it all now—its high towers!! *Cold!! Cruel!! Onimous! Closing down on you!! From every side!* (Wheels stiffly around, pointing in terror) *From every side!!* Till you can't breathe. *Closer! Closer!* (Grabs throat in own grip) Br-a-a-ck-k (Whisper) You can't breathe!! *All day!! All night!* You can't *sleep!! The traffic!* (Hesitates—eyes roll—silence) *Beep-beep! Honk! Honk! Look out for that truck!* Ar-roo-gah!! *Look out for that taxi! Honk! Honk! Boing! Honk! Freep! Breep! Ring-g-g! Honk-beep-beep!* (Quiet) (Sotto voce) Hark—what's that? (Eyes roll, grabs heart, and points up) *Look!* It's the towers! *They're falling!!* (Screams) *Ya-a-h!* (Falls stiffly to ground, arm still pointing up)

PORKY: (Into scene, hands clasped) Why, you poor unsanitary old underprivileged mongrel, you—I-I didn't kn-know—you can stay and get all clean-lived like me—you pathetic sallow creature, you.

CHARLIE: (Looks up) I wanta drink of water, and a cookie, and my very own rubber duck . . . and . . .

And so on.

As was said, if you have Charlie, you don't need Daffy Duck. Charlie is an Old Dog of the Sea, and Sinbad was fortunate beyond his wildest dreams to have had that pleasant interlude with that old man, rather than that young old dog.

At any rate, better it should happen to Porky than to me. I met Charlie when I was old enough and experienced enough to handle him. If I had met a sophisticated self-centered slob like Charlie when I was a child, I most certainly would have turned away from dogs, perhaps pursued a life of canary lover at the very least.

How to Make a Tennis Shoe for a Percheron

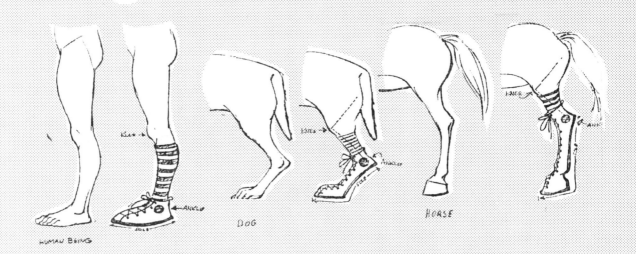

HUMAN BEING   DOG   HORSE

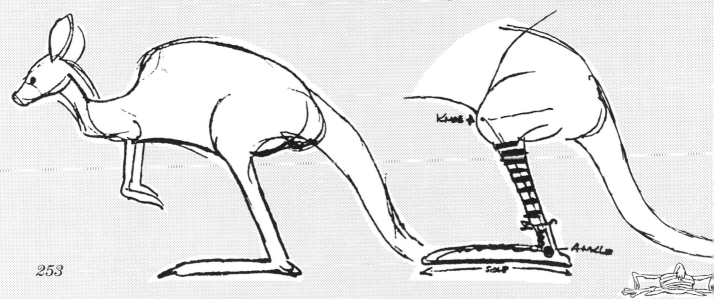

Comparative anatomy as demonstrated by striped socks and basic tennis shoe

Father taught us to swim early—even before he taught us to read. So I learned to swim before I learned to read. The reason for mastering swimming, Father said, was because of his distaste for drowned children. "I never knew a drowned child that was worth much," he said. "Horrid, bloated things, fish-belly white, which, I suppose, is natural enough, since fish, like drowned children, spend a lot of time under-

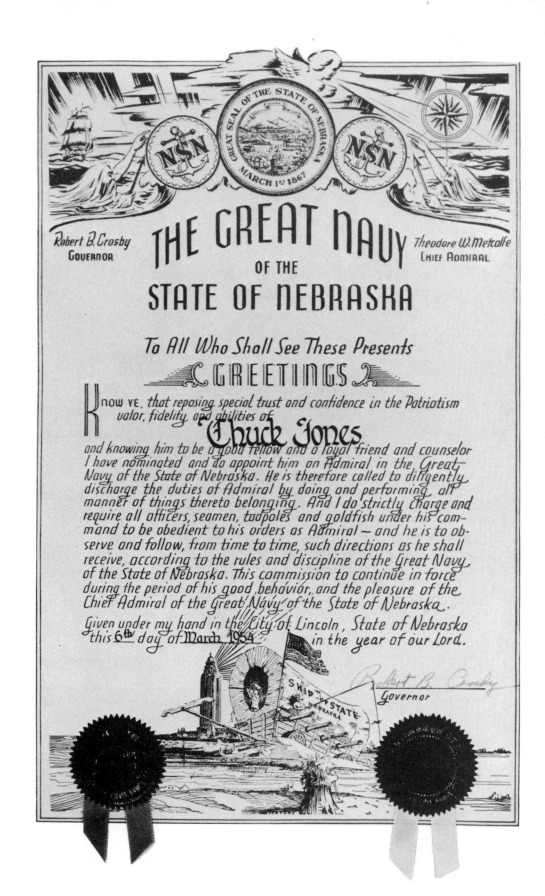

THE GREAT NAVY

OF THE

STATE OF NEBRASKA

Robert B. Crosby
GOVERNOR

Theodore W. Metcalfe
CHIEF ADMIRAL

To All Who Shall See These Presents

GREETINGS

Know ye, that reposing special trust and confidence in the Patriotism, valor, fidelity, and abilities of

Chuck Jones

and knowing him to be a good fellow and a loyal friend and counselor I have nominated and do appoint him an Admiral in the Great Navy of the State of Nebraska. He is therefore called to diligently discharge the duties of Admiral by doing and performing all manner of things thereto belonging. And I do strictly charge and require all officers, seamen, tadpoles and goldfish under his command to be obedient to his orders as Admiral — and he is to observe and follow, from time to time, such directions as he shall receive, according to the rules and discipline of the Great Navy, of the State of Nebraska. This commission to continue in force during the period of his good behavior, and the pleasure of the Chief Admiral of the Great Navy of the State of Nebraska.

Given under my hand in the City of Lincoln, State of Nebraska this 6th day of March, 1954 in the year of our Lord.

Robert B. Crosby
Governor

254

water." Father's distaste for dead moppets was not shared by Huckleberry's friend Jim: "I alwuz liked dead people, en done all I could for 'em"—one of the sweetest and most mysterious statements in English literature.

Father had another simple straightforward statement about the ocean, the only valid one I have ever heard. "The ocean," he said, "doesn't care."

This is all you know about the ocean, and all you need to know. Over the seventy-odd years of my life I have seen the wisdom of this statement many times. I have seen powerful swimmers washed ashore dead in an apparently pacific ocean; I have seen infants carried out to sea by a frothing riptide only to be cast back by a succeeding breaker. I have seen a whale crushed by its own weight on a receding tide, and I have seen a strange and wonderful white mare ride a breaker from straight out to sea—we watched her from among other whitecaps on a wind-tossed autumn day, a mile or so offshore, until she breasted the last wave and galloped off down the beach. I knew then and I know now that she came from Tahiti; I've seen her in Gauguin's paintings.

"The sea," Father repeated, "doesn't care, but *you* do. Heed well." Father often talked like one of the wolves in *The Jungle Book*: "Heed well Louis Pasteur: 'Chance favors the prepared mind.' A cat," he went on, "can adjudge the speed of everything of possible danger to him except an automobile; that's why cats get shot down so often by cars—their minds are not prepared. If you want to be smarter than a cat—which is unlikely prepare your mind and your body for any contingency you can anticipate. It's the lazy person's way—and I do hope you are wise enough to be lazy—so learning to swim is not a sport. Being faster than someone else in the water is silly and ridiculous: a six-year-old child can trot faster than the best swimmer in the world can swim. The only thing you need to know about swimming is how to breathe when you're in the water; if you can breathe, you can swim, and the important thing about swimming is to get where you want or need to go. It may be six feet if you fall into a swimming pool (most children who drown in swimming pools do so within six feet of the deck edge). It may be a mile or so if your boat founders. But one thing is certain: water is an alien element—you *can't* breathe underwater. It's that simple. So, if you want to save my feelings, learn to swim.

"Swimming," my father went on to say, "is a form of transportation. Like walking, it can be done for pleasure. But when you stop walking, you don't ordinarily sink, so never confuse the two."

In 1922 or 1923, Duke Kahanamoku from Hawaii and Haig Priest of Australia had recently landed in Ocean Park with their twelve-foot mahogany surfboards, and surfboarding took root for the first time in America. Body surfing quickly followed, and we all became adept at this wonderful sport. Only strong men could handle the two- and three-hundred-pound boards, so we learned to make our bodies into boards—curling over the wave, not arching against it. To this day, it is a thrill to look down that surging tumble of whitewater and see good friends riding the ocean with you.

Father insisted that we each wear a strong piece of twine around our neck, weighted with a metal amulet. The practical reasoning for this was that if you got caught in a big breaking wave you might, indeed you almost certainly would, find yourself in a great churning snarl of sand and tumbling water, in a vortex not of your own choosing. There is no way of knowing which direction the surface lies; many people in the grip of hysteria and panic have swum *down* to their deaths. "If," Father pointed out, "your amulet is hanging in front of your nose, you will, if you have ordinary intelligence, know that it is pointing down. Gravity," he said, "doesn't lie. If, however, the amulet

Dorothy, Margaret, Richard, and Charles (broken wing) Jones, Balboa, California, 1917

rested against your chest, you were obviously going up, and this," he said, "just might be where the surface lies, and more important, where air can be found."

I was never afraid of sharks. Sea monsters were my dish; I'm still one of the Loch Ness monster's staunchest supporters. In those simple days, the idea of being bitten or devoured by a shark was as remote a possibility as being struck by a bolt of lightning. In fact, people had been struck by lightning on a wet beach in the South Bay—but never then or in the seventy ensuing years has anyone on that thirty-mile stretch ever been touched by a shark. Wait—I stepped on a leopard shark once. Eleven inches long, he was chewing on a piece of seaweed, a vegetarian perhaps, certainly not a clear and present danger.

Yes, we all learned to swim—everything from the classic dogpaddle to the Australian crawl, the stroke that revolutionized swimming. And it got me interested not only in how to swim but in how everybody else swims, culminating many years later in the natural artistry of the sea lion in our filming of Kipling's

"The White Seal" as a half-hour television special. (Sea lions are sometimes mistaken for seals, even by Rudyard Kipling.)

Again, as always, all animals move the way they must move, because their unique anatomy develops as necessary in each unique environment, and the sea lion is no exception.

Since the story "The White Seal" is in the *Bambi* tradition, the characters must move authentically. The sea lions, like the deer in *Bambi*, are humanized only in the sense that they talk to one another. Their strengths and their weaknesses, their problems and their triumphs, are all ultimately conditioned by their unique anatomical structure.

I could not conduct a course in comparative anatomy with my animators. I was not educationally equipped to do so; therefore, I followed the most logical substitute—comparing my own anatomy to that of the sea lion. This is not as difficult as it might sound, since all vertebrates have more structural matters in common than differences. Our bones and muscles all bear pretty much the same names and are readily identifiable; the great differences are primarily in length and weight of the bones and the musculature, and, of course, in the skull structure.

So I went down to the wonderful San Diego Zoo, where I could examine sea lions at their and my leisure, and there they were, as brown as a bunch of movie producers in Palm Springs, only lacking cigars in their fat faces and a bit of colored cloth across their loins to complete the masquerade. Their movements onshore had the same complacent wobble as did many cinematic moguls of that day. Their barks, too, seem to have a similar authoritative ignorance, but once in the water, the sea lion becomes a sinuous master of the aquatic arabesque, a series of grace notes swirling through the water with confident beauty.

And close examination showed that both front and hind flippers had small but very evident toenails. So these were really hands and feet, not fins. It seemed to me that the upper arm-

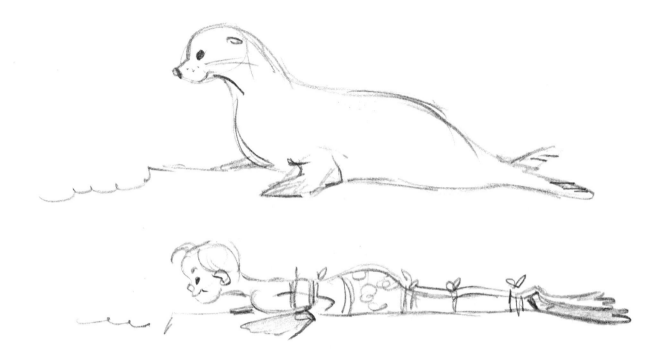

bones, the ulnas, were buried in the body itself but were probably still there; that, in human terms, only the arms from the elbow down were exterior, and the long legbones were also immured inside the long sleek envelope of the body, only the feet emerging as flippers.

Having grandsons of eleven and thirteen, I explained the situation to them and asked their help in demonstrating to my animators how a sea lion *had* to move.

Simplicity itself. I tied their arms to their bodies at the elbow, tied their legs at the knee and ankle, put swim flippers on their feet *and* hands, and threw them into the swimming pool. Within minutes they were swimming the only way they *could* swim—awkwardly, but exactly as a sea lion swims. Even arcing down into the depths and surfacing quickly to breathe. They were as close as a human being could be to a sea lion, and the awkwardness of their movement could easily be corrected by the animator.

Dachshund dolled up as seal

ATTITUDE IS EVERYTHING!

ELMER   BUGS   DAFFY   PEVE   PORKY

Comparative anatomy is a vital tool of the complete animator or director. What he looks for is *not* how another creature is different but how he is the same—an example is what I call the tennis-shoe proof. If one ascertains where the toe bones, heels, and ankles of a horse, a dog, and a man are, and then creates a tennis shoe to fit that structure, the comparisons become relatively easy and the movement more easily understood.

This kind of analysis is only necessary when you are animating

Same bones—different lengths only

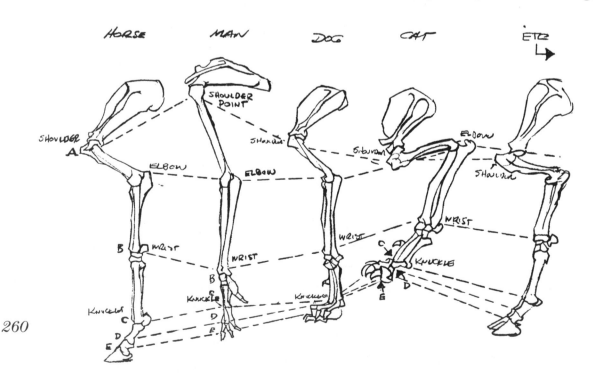

HORSE   MAN   DOG   CAT   ETC

260

FOGHORN   HENRY   TWEETY   SYLVESTER

Running attitudes are as diverse as are our characters

animals as they appear. With Bugs, Daffy, etc., we invented our own anatomical structures and were faithful to them. And, speaking of comparative anatomy, let me lay to rest for all time—a big order, but one easily demonstrated—that when we animated Bugs, Daffy, and Co., we animated "realistically" or "academically," compared to the deeply intellectual "abstractions" of some of the so-called avant-garde animators of what I call the American and European Plight-of-Man school.

If our work was academic, so, let it be said, was Picasso's. Our characters are based on individual personalities, their anatomy abstracted only in the most general way from their prototypes—rabbits, ducks, cats, canaries, etc.

We must all start with the believable. That is the essence of our craft. All drama, all comedy, all artistry stems from the believable, which gives us as solid a rock as anyone could ask from which to seek humor: variations on the believable—that is the essence of all humor. We can be even more precise. Yes, humor is always based on human behavior. In animation this is clearly demonstrated. All great cartoon characters are based on human behavior we recognize in ourselves.

Characters *always* came first, before the physical representation. Just as it is with all living things, including human beings. We are not what we look like. We are not even what we sound like.

And so it was and is with Bugs and Daffy, Elmer, Porky,

COYOTE   ROAD RUNNER   YOSEMITE SAM

and Pepé Le Pew. What they look like grew in each case from our discovery of *who* they were. Then and only then could their movements and voices uniquely demonstrate each of these personalities. And as it is with human beings, the voice does not make the character. The character develops the kind of voice necessary to express his individuality.

Animated characters grow and evolve, just as human beings do. Perhaps Bugs Bunny in his earliest appearances somewhat resembled Harpo Marx. After which he passed through a Woody Woodpecker stage (before Woody), on to a Groucho Marx stage, and finally settled comfortably down into a quiet-living rabbit, similar, as pointed out earlier, to Rex Harrison as Professor Higgins, with overtones of Dorothy Parker playing D'Artagnan. Left to his own devices, Bugs would doubtless live a life of contemplation and pursue intellectual matters. But, as in the case of most of us, the society around him seems dedicated to contradicting his wishes and ambitions. Seemingly secure in his rabbitat, he is constantly accosted by enemies bent on doing him hurt, or sending him off in rockets, exposing him to the enmities of fanatics like Yosemite Sam, whose simple hatred of all rabbits creates conflict.

But once the battle has started, once provoked, our quiet-living rabbit becomes a living terror, and happily and cheerfully joins the conflict. "Of course you realize this means war" is not an idle statement.

262

All our characters are recognizable not only by their personal characteristics but by how they express these characteristics in response to conflict or love or any adversarial situation.

So, in the same or similar situation, each will respond in a unique and typical fashion. This is where the challenge, the fun, and the professionalism of the artist or the animator come into play—a challenge not to be taken lightly by anyone.

The great wonder of animation is not the illusion of life but life itself. Our characters achieve believability *because* of their limitations. As mentioned earlier:

There is no such thing as sympathy without believability; there is no such thing as real laughter without sympathy.

Developing an animated character is very much like getting married. You must learn how to get along together, and you must show great patience and understanding about what you can and what you cannot do, to bring the individual best out in each character, be it Bugs, Daffy, or any other of the characters we developed at Warner Bros.

When you are engaged in full animation, or in character live-action comedy, the character takes over, pushes you aside; you become the interpreter of his actions. You are no more a cartoonist in the static sense than Chaplin was a still photographer. You respond to another personality, moving it as it *needs* to go—as it *must* go. Drawing becomes as unconscious a necessity to you as body mechanics are unconscious to the dancer during the performance. You cannot practice mechanics during a performance, because you are now the life force, the moving response. You *are* the interpreter of actions which surprise both you and the character you vitalize; you and he together become the series of surprises that is animation.

As you develop any character, you are, of course, looking into a mirror, a reflection of yourself, your ambitions and hopes, your realizations and fears. Chaplin could only have found the

Retitled ODOR-ABLE KITTY *(1945)*

STINKY
1018
"FOREVER
AMBUSHED"

264

Little Tramp within himself. Gazing at or trying to analyze other tramps would have done him no good at all. There is that little tramp in all of us; it takes a great artist to bring it fully to the surface where we can all recognize it. Just so with Daffy and Bugs and Elmer and Tweety Bird and Yosemite Sam. If there was comic artistry at our studio, it formed itself into these varied aspects of the human character through group effort or, rather, through unconscious group effort. But it could be brought to final and unique life as an individual only by an individual, and that individual responsibility rested on the director.

Like the Little Tramp, there is a self-serving, the-world-owes-me-a-living, I-want-not-only-my-share-but-a-reasonably-greater-share-than-you Daffy Duck in all of us. Just as there is an I'm-going-to-only-if-you-interfere-with-my-shooting-wabbits appeal to the audience, and as a Grinch hates Christmas, so Yosemite Sam, who hates rabbits, arouses in us a sympathy. We'd all like the freedom to seriously, loudly, honestly, publicly state our hatred of something. Pepé Le Pew presented no problem to me. I *needed* his self-assurance, his absolute certainty of his male desirability, his calm self-assurance, his logical interpretation of any female peccadillo as simply a loving way to convey her love for him. So Pepé was not a recognition in myself of his wonderful attributes but an absolute recognition in myself of the absence of those traits. I *needed* Pepé in the same way that I needed Bugs (nothing heroic in my mirror). In high school I was not only a wimp, I was a wimp-nerd-nebbish. I was 6'1" and weighed 132 pounds. I was transparent to the other sex; girls could look through me to admire other boys.

You see, that's the whole wonder of animation directing. If you're not something you want to be, or *are* something you don't want to be, you can, through drawing, through action, create a character who will take care of the matter. All you need to do is dig down into your cluttered cellar of frustration or up into your cluttered attic of ambition and lo—there you are! Leering, smiling, crouching, sneering, or hoping from behind the furniture. It takes tugging, threats, and promises to lure the character you want to the surface, but once there, it suddenly takes on a life of its own and starts chatting and acting away in its own surprising way. "Do not come wiz me to ze Casbah," says Pepé. "We shall makes beyootiful musics togezzer *right here*." A perfectly sensible and absolutely logical attitude to take. You are the corn-beef, I am the cabbage, he assures his paramour, and as she flees: "Ze cab-baj do not run away from ze corn-beef!!" Well, of course, it doesn't, and in my luscious sexual dreams, girls did not run away from me, nor, far, far worse than this, did they ignore me. Indifference and humiliation. These are the bête noire of all human beings. Well, as a girl you couldn't ignore Pepé Le Pew, and if you did, he wouldn't recognize it.

So, Pepé and Bugs are comic heroes, and precious few of them there are in live action or in animation. It is not just happenchance that those comedians we love the most and laugh at the longest are those who sympathetically portray our own mistakes, mishaps, and stumblings, and perhaps, subliminally, reassure us by demonstrating through that laughter that we are not alone.

Jack Benny, who supposedly had the devious crabby, miserly personality of Uriah Heep, yet moved with elegant contrast and the gallant bodily gestures of a cavalier, should have known how great a comedian he was. Yet one day he said, "I have this clinging fear that someday, someone is going to shake me into reality, and I'll find it just isn't so, that I'm not funny, that no one can conceivably laugh at or with me."

In that sense, if *only* in that sense, I am at one with all great comedians.

"And now, chérie, I shull tell you everything about skunks you were afraid to ask"

It has been said that our characters are realistic . . . Well . . .

RABBIT -

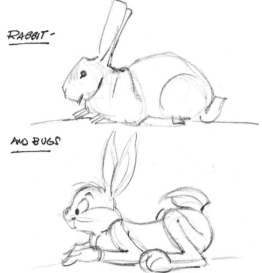

AND BUGS

DUCK AND DAFFY DUCK

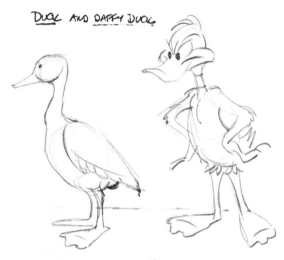

THIS IS NO MORE A NATURAL
POSITION FOR BUGS THAN IT
WOULD BE FOR A HUMAN BEING
— BUT, I'M TRYING TO BE FAIR.

— THERE IS A CERTAIN SIMILARITY
IN FOOT STRUCTURE — AND NEITHER
OF THEM WEARS GLOVES

CAT AND SYLVESTER

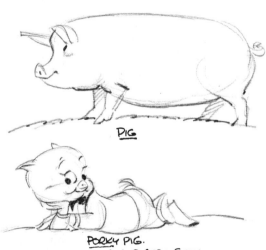

PIG

PORKY PIG.
— THE TAIL IS A DIRECT STEAL.

THE EARS DO LOOK SOMETHING ALIKE
EVEN THOUGH THERE IS A PAINFUL
DISCREPANCY IN THE NOSES.

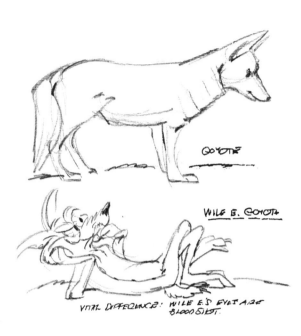

COYOTE

WILE E. COYOTE

VITAL DIFFERENCE: WILE E.'S EYES ARE
BLOODSHOT.

ROADRUNNER
(GEOCOCCYX CALIFORNIANUS) (HOTROADICUS SUPERSONICUS)

TASMANIAN DEVIL   TASMANIAN DEVIL

—THEY ARE BOTH FROM TASMANIA

WELL- THEY BOTH HAVE
WINGS AND EYES AND......

A   P   P   E

A human appendix can usually be removed, if a source of irritation, without seriously endangering the body. I suspect this is equally true of a book. Therefore, this appendix is included for those who find more stability for themselves in following the chronology of the author's life. This is the reader's inalienable right and I have no intention of disputing it.

I was born in Spokane, Washington, U.S.A., on September 21, 1912. Apparently I became bored, and emigrated to Southern California at the age of six months, accompanied on this journey by my father, Charles Adams Jones; my mother, Mabel Martin Jones; and two sisters, Margaret Barbara Jones and Dorothy Jane Jones. A brother, Richard Kent Jones, joined the procession later, and these siblings corralled a substantial and unfair portion of the cerebral matter allocated to the Jones family.

I received a sketchy but catholic (not Catholic) education in California and as a high school dropout at the age of fifteen attended Chouinard Art Institute (now California Institute of the Arts), graduating without distinction or the ability to draw. After ten ensuing years of night school, with the help of the great teacher Donald Graham, I still could not draw but could now fake it fairly well.

So, in 1930, after art school, I found work in a commercial art studio and also found out that drawing was no particular

Cowpoke Jones, on the right, in the Rose Parade, 1929

advantage in the field of commercial art. After being thrown out of commercial art forever, I found in 1931 an occupation that was ideal: cel(luloid) washing. As a promising cel washer I was discovered by Ub Iwerks, who had just started his own studio after leaving Walt Disney. I washed cels of *Flip the Frog* with distinction and alacrity and began my long climb to mediocrity by becoming successively a cel painter, a cel inker, and eventually an in-betweener, now called an assistant animator,

C. Jones and associates:
Walt Lantz Studio, 1932

C.J., at time of wedding to
Dorothy Webster, 1935

from which lofty post I was immediately fired—Mr. Iwerks recognizing the Peter Principle even then: that a good cel washer could be promoted to a singularly incapable in-betweener.

In the same year, after brief sorties with Charles Mintz and Walt Lantz, neither of whom wanted cel washers in-betweening, I returned to the Iwerks studio, where I was unrecognized, but my work unfortunately was. And I was fired again, this time by Ub's secretary, Dorothy Webster, a sociology graduate from the University of Oregon (who later, in 1935, became my wife, probably on the wan supposition that a good cel washer might also be a good dishwasher).

Carrying my credentials under my arm, I shipped out before the mast, calling myself Ishmael and hoping to find a cel-washing factory in Central America, but the large schooner intelligently caught fire and burned to the waterline, leaving me with a suit of long red underwear and one tennis shoe to face the world.

Feeling rightly that my haberdashery fitted me for the life of a bohemian (hippie), I moved into the artists' section of Olvera

1933

1937

*Bob Clampett's recognition
of C.J.'s fatherhood*

*Top echelon and wives:
nature of celebration
obscured by time; C.J.
third from left in top row,
Dorothy directly in front
of me*

Street in Los Angeles and worked as a maladroit puppeteer and portrait artist ($1 a throw—a grotesque overcharge).

After a year of this, having had to refund ninety cents on the dollar on about 85 percent of the portraits, I felt the need for greater security and proposed to Dorothy Webster, who was still working steady and had saved up $3 for a future marriage license. (She didn't have to worry about my Wassermann test—since at 6′1″ and 135 pounds I had received few offers of lechery.)

Dorothy then proved herself perfidious by obtaining a job for me with Leon Schlesinger, who had just split off from his directors, Hugh Harman and Rudolph Ising, to form his own studio. (In a way, this was a good turn for Hugh and Rudy, who discovered that Harman-Ising was probably a more appealing name for a cartoon studio than Leon Schlesinger Productions.)

Since Leon Schlesinger did not draw, he didn't know the

*Art Heineman: brilliant
character designer*

difference between a cel washer and an in-betweener, and I,
finally knowing a good thing when I saw it, remained in those
cloistered halls most of my adult life (1933–63). By the time
Mr. Edward Selzer took over command when Leon Schlesinger
sold out to Warner Bros., I had floated up by way of animating
to directing: the first time a cel washer had accomplished this
without detection. Mr. Selzer, who did not know a director
from a hole-in-the-ground, supposed me to be a hole, and
treated me accordingly.

As an in-betweener I had worked (if the term can be used
loosely) for Ham Hamilton, who then forced me into animation
to get me off in-betweening for him. This was on the Buddy
series directed by Jack King and Earl Herd, and fortunately
nothing in the way of bad animation could make Buddy worse
than he was anyway. Then the brilliant Friz Freleng moved
over from Harman-Ising, and Mr. Freleng could easily tell the
difference between a hole-in-the-ground and a hole-in-the-head
and put up no resistance whatsoever when Bob Clampett and
I were assigned to the newly formed Tex Avery unit, housed
in an ancient bungalow faintly redolent of early Norma Talmadge
and known accurately and affectionately as Termite Terrace.
The prime product of Termite Terrace, beside termites, was
Porky Pig and the beginnings of the wildly insane version of
Daffy Duck.

*Ham Hamilton: my first
animator*

My admiration for the art of Friz Freleng and Tex Avery
was and is boundless. Both were masters of timing, faultless
gag structure, and a kind of nutty believability. Being exposed
over a long period of time to genius was bound to have its
effect—even on an accomplished cel washer.

Poor Ub Iwerks! In a bad financial moment for him, Mr.
Schlesinger came to his financial aid—it turned out to be a
takeover—but as a penalty sent Mr. Clampett and me to Ub's
studio to act as child co-directors on a series called Gabby Goat.

Fat Jones, circa 1942

By some peculiar alchemy I do not yet understand, the co-directorship disappeared and I found myself animating for Bob Clampett.

The highly competent Henry Binder, business manager for Leon Schlesinger, a man who could not bear to see dumb animals suffer, in one of his few faulty moments rescued me and put me in as a director of the Frank Tashlin unit, Mr. Tashlin having lost interest in animation. (He was to go on to become an immensely successful live-action writer, director, and producer.)

With some help from my wife, I produced a daughter, Linda, in 1937. Linda, in 1989, is now Linda Jones Clough, the manager, president, majordomo, and prime mover of the Jones enterprises, which consist of Linda Jones Enterprises and Chuck Jones Enterprises, producing, preserving, and authenticating drawings and cels from my past, present, and future, selling them through major art galleries in the United States, including the Circle Fine Art Galleries and Gallery Lainzberg. In my eyes—and whose other eyes can I trust?—she had always been a perfect daughter and now is helping to bring animation art out of the pit that it was in for so long: Disney *gave away* cels in the first year or so of Disneyland. Cels have sold at Christie's today for over $100,000.

C.J. and daughter, Linda, 1989

Lobby cards of early C.J.
films: THE NIGHT WATCHMAN
(1938), THE DOVER BOYS
(1942), FOX POP *(1942)*

My first directorial achievement was *The Night Watchman* in 1938, followed by some films about dogs, mice, and bats, and some of the first and worst Bugs Bunnies. In 1940 I won the Newsreel Theatre's award for the best animated cartoon of the year, a patriotic cartoon called *Old Glory*. This award was unique in that it was never given before or since and was the first such award to be won by a cel washer.

During the war years I collaborated (there must be a better word) with Theodor Geisel (Dr. Seuss) on a goof-up soldier named Private Snafu. ("Snafu" can be translated any way you please, but the first words are *S*ituation *N*ormal . . .) Almost twenty-five years later this writer-director team would produce *How the Grinch Stole Christmas* and *Horton Hears a Who*. These two films won the Peabody Award for Television Programming

274

*Chuck Jones, Dick
Thompson, Ken Harris,
and talented layout man*

Excellence, an award that *has* been given before and since.

In 1942 I directed *The Dover Boys*, considered by many animators, including the wonderfully talented John Hubley, to have helped set the style, method, and timing for much of the animation to follow. Along with John McGrew, Bernyce Polifka, and Eugene Fleury, I was also experimenting with highly stylized, formalized backgrounds in such films as *Fox Pop, Bugs Bunny and the Three Bears*, and *The Aristo Cat*. That's right, *The Aristo Cat*, in 1943. I was able to steal it from the Disney studio twenty years before they deftly added an "s" to *The Aristocats*. This is what is known as retroactive plagiarism on my part.

In 1944, working nights, I directed without compensation *Hell Bent for Election*, because of my love for F.D.R. This was the first full-length UPA short.

After the war, I began my long association with Mike Maltese, writer; Maurice Noble and Phil De Guard, layout and background; and that superb crew of animators: Ken Harris, Ben Washam, Phil Monroe, Abe Levitow, Lloyd Vaughan, and Dick Thompson. In the next twenty-five years together we

Relative sizes of our unit's animators and animated characters

276

discovered the Road Runner and Coyote, Pepé Le Pew, Michigan J. Frog, the Three Bears, Hubie and Bertie, etc., and shared, mainly with Friz Freleng and Robert McKimson, the character and drawing development of Bugs Bunny, Daffy Duck, Elmer Fudd, Porky Pig, and many others.

Films by this unit won two Academy Awards in 1950: *For Scent-imental Reasons*, with Pepé Le Pew, and the documentary award for the Public Health Service, *So Much for So Little* (co-written with Friz Freleng), the first and only time an animated short has won in the documentary category.

In 1955 I had a four-month stint at Disney when Mr. Jack Warner, responding to the obvious logic that all films would soon be 3-D and that all babies would soon be born with one green and one red retina, closed the Warner cartoon plant.

Mr. Warner's insight fortunately proved to be slightly flawed in logic and the Warner cartoon plant inhaled and exhaled again, only to go permanently rigor as well as mortis in 1962.

I have always fancied myself a lay scientist (as well as a lay astronomer, lay zoologist, and lay man) and directed during those fading years the cartoon sequences in *Gateways to the Mind*, a television special for the Bell Telephone Company dealing with the human senses. I was surprised to find that a good case can be made for only one sense, that of touch, or an equally good case can be made for 100 or more individual responses—such as pressure, heat, cold, etc.: so much for the five senses.

In 1962 Dorothy and I wrote an original story and screenplay for UPA, *Gay Purr-ee*, with the voices of Judy Garland, Robert Goulet, Hermione Gingold, and Red Buttons, and directed by Abe Levitow.

After leaving Warners, or rather, as reported earlier, having Warners pulled out from under me, I did a little oil and water-color painting and drawing and sold some of these objets d'art

Lithograph: Daffy Duck on
DECEMBER MORN

at the Cowie and Manhattan Galleries to gullible friends who probably didn't know paintings from a hole-in-the-ground. Most of the paintings had been done in Europe anyway, the styles stolen from obscure artists unlikely to be recognized in America. Today I am again engaged in easel painting, depicting in oils Bugs Bunny, Daffy Duck, Porky Pig, etc., in rank imitation of the masters.

Early in 1964, M-G-M for some reason wanted some more Tom 'n' Jerrys and couldn't afford Hanna and Barbera, who had originated the series. So I rallied my old crew around me and produced some Tom 'n' Jerrys, and also Frank Tashlin's *The Bear That Wasn't*, Walt Kelly's *The Pogo Family Birthday Special*, and *The Dot and the Line*, which won an Academy Award in 1965, as well as *How the Grinch Stole Christmas* and *Horton Hears a Who* with Dr. Seuss.

During this time at M-G-M I also produced, co-directed, and co-authored the screenplay for *The Phantom Tollbooth*, a full-length feature. A critical success, a box-office question mark. *Tollbooth* keeps resurfacing on call from film festivals (FILMEX in Los Angeles; Deauville in France) and has been recently issued as a home videocassette.

For a year I was a vice president of the American Broadcasting Company, hoping to help the cause of children's television programming. With the help of the National Film Board of Canada, the Zagreb Studios, and many talented cartoonists such as Johnny Hart, Don Arioli of the National Film Board, and Hank Ketcham, *Curiosity Shop* was produced: a seventeen-unit one-hour program for Saturday morning. The program can be described in a kindly way as highly ordinary, but it did establish in my porous but not always selective mind that short subjects and television specials were better arenas for talented cel washers and that seventeen anythings a year was beyond my powers. Perhaps, in the light of the shows now disfiguring Saturday-morning television, beyond anyone's powers.

At this time I also served as executive producer for Charles

Lithograph: Bugs Bunny as Chagall would have painted him

Dickens's *A Christmas Carol*, done in toto by the incredibly talented Richard Williams in London. My creative contribution was to find a sponsor and a network.

Today I am once again with Warner Bros. as a consultant and roving front man.

In 1962 I established my own independent production company, Chuck Jones Enterprises. Chuck Jones Enterprises produced nine half-hour prime-time television specials, all produced, written, and directed by me. They are: *The Cricket in Times Square, A Very Merry Cricket,* and *Yankee Doodle Cricket* (for ABC); three stories from Rudyard Kipling's *The Jungle Book—Rikki-Tikki-Tavi, Mowgli's Brothers* (both of which received the Parents' Choice Awards in 1985), and *The White Seal* (for CBS); two specials populated by

C.J. at his Tower 12 Studio

some of the classic characters from Warner Bros., *Carnival of the Animals* (Daffy Duck and Bugs Bunny playing the music of Saint-Saëns and reading the verse of Ogden Nash) and *A Connecticut Rabbit in King Arthur's Court* (the Warner Bros. gang in a tale "plagiarized from Mark Twain" and later titled *Bugs Bunny in King Arthur's Court*). Both were aired on CBS. Also for CBS: *Raggedy Ann and Andy in: The Great Santa Claus Caper*, and *The Pumpkin Who Couldn't Smile*, in which I took the classic Johnny Gruelle characters on winter and Halloween adventures, and added a Raggedy dog called, for some reason, Raggedy Arthur.

In 1978 Dorothy Webster Jones, friend, critic, writer, dance partner, wonderful mother and grandmother, died after a lifetime of support, encouragement, and love to animation, to her husband, and to life itself, leaving three splendid grandchildren: Todd, Craig, and Valerie Kausen, and now three great-grandchildren, Alexander and Brittany to Craig and his wife, Mary, and Jessica to Todd and his wife, Jan.

Great great-grandchildren!

*Brittany
(Craig and Mary)*

*Alexander
(Craig and Mary)*

*Jessica
(Todd and Jan)*

Grand grandchildren!

Valerie, Craig, and Todd Kausen, 1967

Same group, same pose, 1989

Another Soviet cartoonist tries his hand at portraiture

The teaching situation in the United States is best exemplified by reporting that I have lectured and conducted workshops at Stanford University, the University of Kansas, the University of Iowa, Johns Hopkins, the Universities of California and Nevada, San Francisco State College, Art Center College of Design in Pasadena, Cal Arts, USC, UCLA, and many others. The University of California at Santa Cruz conducted an accredited course on my films, under the direction of Tim Hunter. You wouldn't think there would be that much interest in cel washing. I have also been honored for some reason by a three-day retrospective at London's British Film Institute, twice at the Kennedy Film Center, by the American Film Institute, and

282

C.J.'s drawings on the wall of the Museum of Modern Art, New York

by other backward cultural centers such as Toronto, Zagreb, Montreal. I am a Regents Lecturer at the University of California at La Jolla and Visiting Lecturer at Cambridge University, England, and Guardian Lecturer in England also.

For CBS I produced *Daffy Duck's Thanks-for-Giving Special*, which includes the segment *Duck Dodgers in the Return of the 24½ Century* and also *Bugs Bunny's Bustin' Out All Over*; and three separate cartoons, including *Portrait of the Artist As a Young Rabbit*.

A *Film Comment* magazine issue devoted to "The Hollywood Cartoon" carried two articles on me and my cartoons by Greg Ford and Richard Thompson, whose combined encyclopedic knowledge of my cartoons baffles me. *Time* magazine film critic Jay Cocks featured a full-page article on me. If I was alive I would have been utterly delighted with just the opening line: "He has made moviegoers laugh as often and as well as Keaton or Chaplin." A recent United States Information Agency magazine, printed in Russian for distribution in the U.S.S.R., features an article on my work. For the record, the name Chuck in Russian comes out "Yuk."

I have a recently published children's book, *William, the Backwards Skunk*, published by Crown in early 1987.

I have turned a penchant for lassitude into a vocation in my declining years (I decline most work offers) and at present have but a few immediate projects: a new book, *How to Draw from the Fun Side of Your Brain*, showing how to construct all the major Warner Bros. characters, including over a thousand drawings plus biographies of each character; and I continue to make special drawings and paintings for daughter Linda's business, all of which keeps me at a safe level of lassitude.

My dotage has been enlivened by the unexpected: a Golden Anniversary Salute to Warner Bros. Animation by the New York Museum of Modern Art in September 1985, honoring Friz

Working on the mural requested by the Museum of the Moving Image, London, 1988

Freleng, Mel Blanc, and the subject of this unvarnished biography; by unwarranted written praise and showings from such disparate sources as Dartmouth College, UCLA, London, Deauville, Belgium, Toronto, Quebec, Montreal, Miami, Dallas; by the Telluride Film Festival (where I was honored as part of a troika consisting of King Vidor, King Kong, and me . . . known in some quarters as the six of clubs).

All this should be taken with a grain of salt the size of an armadillo, keeping an awareness at all times of the truth that "It is not necessary to deserve something in order to enjoy it."

I do not deserve Marian J. Dern Jones, but I enjoy her love with just as much surprise as my press notices evoke incredibility. We were married in January 1983, whereupon she reassumed her maiden name, which happened to be Jones. She is a writer of singular ability, and has been film critic for a Beverly Hills newspaper, a national staff writer for *TV Guide*, and a scriptwriter for TV and the comic strip "Rick O'Shay and Hipshot," as well as for several of my TV specials. She has a son, Peter, a daughter, Rosalin, and three young grandsons.

We are incurable travelers, having made our way via ship,

*Beloved wife caught beautifully
by Yousuf Karsh*

*The old grey hair
and the old grey hare*

AH AIN'T READY TO
GO YET, BOY. AH AIN'T
BEEN BUFFETED!

EXIT

train, car, plane, and helicopter through Great Britain and Europe, Australia, Japan, Mexico, Canada—without being denied entry to any country so far. We dance at the drop of a quarter note, and quite beautifully so, a triumph of her grace and ability over my two left feet. And we ramble as joyfully as children along the Pacific beaches, a few hundred feet from our back door.

Perhaps the most accurate remark about me was uttered by Ray Bradbury at his fifty-fifth birthday party. In answer to the usual question: "What do you want to be when you grow up?" Ray replied: "I want to be fourteen years old like Chuck Jones."

Perhaps this will be my most apt possible epitaph.

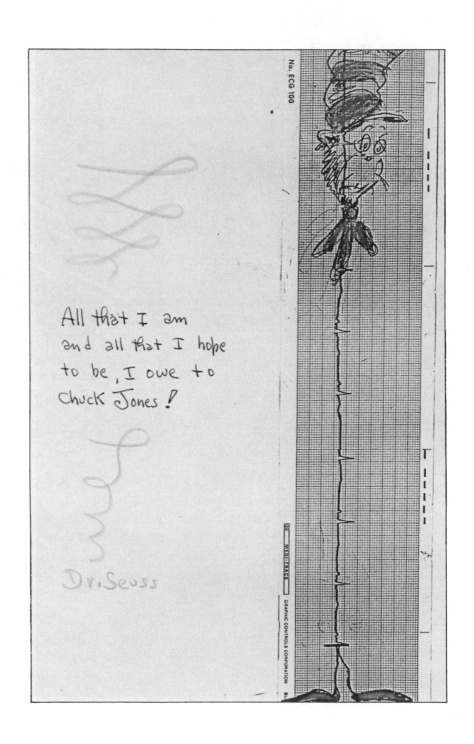

All that I am
and all that I hope
to be, I owe to
Chuck Jones!

Dr. Seuss

Ted (Dr. Seuss) Geisel,
Boris Karloff, and C.J.
recording HOW THE GRINCH
STOLE CHRISTMAS *(1967)*
(Peabody Award winner)

Bobe Cannon by C.J.

Norton Juster (author),
C.J., and Robert Morley
recording THE DOT AND THE
LINE *(1965; Academy Award winner)*

C. Jones and Jim Henson,
London, 1988

Theodor (Dr. Seuss) Geisel and associate, 1989

Jones and Robin Williams,
Telluride, Colorado Film
Festival, 1987

288

C. Jones and friend

289

Walt Kelly and Todd Kausen, THE POGO FAMILY BIRTHDAY SPECIAL *(1971)*

The ultimate tribute from Walt Kelly, 1971

Walt Kelly,
Todd Kausen
. . . and C. Jones

290

Marian wrote this comic strip for several years; this Sunday issue came out on my birthday

Animation desk and painting area, Corona del Mar, 1989

What language is this?

The ultimate salutes from Herblock, the greatest editorial cartoonist of our time

Mike Peters gets into the act . . .

CARTOON REST HOME

and again . . .

3-17

and again—bless his heart

REMEMBERING DOROTHY WEBSTER JONES
1907–78

Who supplied the $3 necessary for our marriage in 1935 and who supplied the courage, patience, honesty, and love I so needed for forty years thereafter. Her devotion and the wonderful mother she was are evident in the wonderful daughter and grandchildren and great-grandchildren she left.

I regret that she could not have lived to see what superb great-grandchildren have followed—all of whom have her beauty, curiosity, and sense of wonder.

FILMOGRAPHY

1938

The Night Watchman

1939

Dog Gone Modern
Robin Hood Makes Good
Prest-o Change-o

Daffy Duck and the Dinosaur
Naughty but Mice
Old Glory
Snow Man's Land
Little Brother Rat
Little Lion Hunter
The Good Egg
Sniffles and the Bookworm
Curious Puppy

1940

The Mighty Hunters
Elmer's Candid Camera
Sniffles Takes a Trip
Tom Thumb in Trouble
The Egg Collector
Ghost Wanted
Stage Fright
Good Night Elmer
Bedtime for Sniffles

1941

Elmer's Pet Rabbit
Sniffles Bells the Cat
Joe Glow, the Firefly
Toy Trouble
Porky's Ant
Porky's Prize Pony
Inki and the Lion
Snow Time for Comedy
Brave Little Bat
Saddle Silly
Porky's Midnight Matinee

1942

The Bird Came C.O.D.
Porky's Cafe
Conrad the Sailor
Dog Tired
The Draft Horse
Hold the Lion, Please!
The Squawkin' Hawk
Fox Pop
The Dover Boys
My Favorite Duck
Case of the Missing Hare

1943

To Duck or Not to Duck
Flop Goes the Weasel
Super-Rabbit
The Unbearable Bear
The Aristo Cat
Wackiki Wabbit
Fin N' Catty
Inki and the Mynah Bird

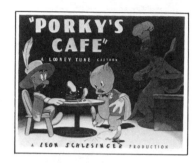

1944

Tom Turk and Daffy
Bugs Bunny and the Three Bears
The Weakly Reporter
Angel Puss
From Hand to Mouse
Lost and Foundling
Hell Bent for Election

1945

Odor-able Kitty
Trap Happy Porky
Hare Conditioned
Fresh Airedale
Hare Tonic

1946

Quentin Quail
Hush My Mouse
Hair-Raising Hare
The Eager Beaver
Fair and Worm-er
Roughly Squeaking

1947

Scent-imental Over You
Inki at the Circus
A Pest in the House
Little Orphan Airedale

1948

A Feather in His Hare
What's Brewin' Bruin?
Rabbit Punch
Haredevil Hare
You Were Never Duckier
House-Hunting Mice
Daffy Dilly
My Bunny Lies Over the Sea
Scaredy Cat

1949

Awful Orphan
Mississippi Hare
Mouse Wreckers
The Bee-Deviled Bruin
Long-Haired Hare
Often an Orphan
Fast and Furry-ous
Frigid Hare
For Scent-imental Reasons
Bear Feat
Rabbit Hood

1950

The Scarlet Pumpernickel
Homeless Hare
The Hypo-chondri-cat
Eight Ball Bunny
Dog Gone South
The Ducksters
Caveman Inki
Rabbit of Seville
Two's a Crowd

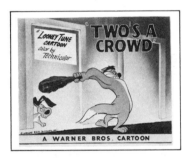

1951

Bunny Hugged
Scent-imental Romeo
A Hound for Trouble
Rabbit Fire
Chow Hound
The Wearing of the Grin
Cheese Chasers
A Bear for Punishment
Dripalong Daffy

1952

Operation: Rabbit
Feed the Kitty
Little Beau Pepe
Water, Water Every Hare
Beep, Beep
The Hasty Hare
Going! Going! Gosh!
Mouse Warming
Rabbit Seasoning
Terrier Stricken

1953

Don't Give Up the Sheep
Forward March Hare
Kiss Me Cat
Duck Amuck
Much Ado About Nutting
Wild Over You
Duck Dodgers in the 24½ Century
Bully for Bugs
Zipping Along
Duck! Rabbit! Duck!
Punch Trunk

1954

Feline Frame-Up
No Barking
Cat's Bah
Claws for Alarm
Bewitched Bunny
Stop, Look and Hasten
From A to Z-Z-Z-Z
Lumber Jack-Rabbit
My Little Duckaroo
Sheep Ahoy
Baby Buggy Bunny

1955

Beanstalk Bunny
Ready, Set, Zoom!
Past Perfumance
Rabbit Rampage
Double or Mutton
Jumpin' Jupiter
Knight-Mare Hare
Two Scents Worth
Guided Muscle
One Froggy Evening

1956

Bugs Bonnets
Broom-Stick Bunny
Rocket Squad
Heaven Scent
Gee Whiz-z-z-z
Barbary Coast Bunny
Rocket-Bye Baby
Deduce, You Say
There They Go-Go-Go
To Hare Is Human

1957

Scrambled Aches
Ali Baba Bunny
Go Fly a Kit
Boyhood Daze
Steal Wool
What's Opera, Doc?
Zoom and Bored
Touche and Go

1958

Robin Hood Daffy
Hare Way to the Stars
Whoa, Be Gone!
To Itch His Own
Hook, Line and Stinker
Hip Hip—Hurry
Cat Feud

1959

Baton Bunny
   (codirector Abe Levitow)
Hot Rod and Reel
Really Scent
Wild About Hurry

1960

The Fastest with the Mostest
Who Scent You?
Rabbit's Feat
Ready Woolen and Able
Hopalong Casualty
High Note

1961

Zip 'N' Snort
The Mouse on 57th Street
The Abominable Snow Rabbit
Lickety Splat
A Scent of the Matterhorn
Compressed Hare
Beep Prepared
Nelly's Folly

1962

A Sheep in the Deep
Zoom at the Top
Louvre Come Back to Me
Martian Through Georgia
   (codirector Abe Levitow)

*Academy Award
nomination, 1961*

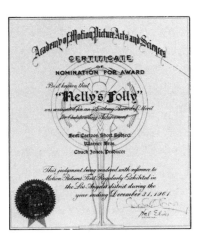

1963

I Was a Teenage Thumb
Now Hear This
Woolen Under Where
   (codirectors Phil Monroe
   and Richard Thompson)
Hare-Breadth Hurry
Mad as a Mars Hare
Transylvania 6-5000
To Beep or Not to Beep

*Nelly, the Yma Sumac of
the jungle:* NELLY'S FOLLY *(1961)*

1964

War and Pieces
The Cat Above, the Mouse Below
Is There a Doctor in the Mouse?
Much Ado About Mousing
Snowbody Loves Me
Unshrinkable Jerry Mouse

1965

The Dot and the Line
Ah—Sweet Mouse Story of Life
Tom-ic Energy
Bad Day at Cat Rock
The Brothers Carry-Mouse-Off
Haunted Mouse
I'm Just Wild About Jerry
Of Feline Bondage
Tom Thump
The Year of the Mouse
The Cat's Me-Ouch
Jerry Go-Round

1966

Duel Personality
Jerry Jerry Quite Contrary
Love Me, Love My Mouse

1967

The Bear That Wasn't
Cat and Duplicat
Cannery Rodent
How the Grinch Stole Christmas [*TV special*]
Gillette commercial

1971

The Phantom Tollbooth [*Feature*]
Horton Hears a Who [*TV special*]
The Pogo Family Birthday Special [*TV special*]

1972

Curiosity Shop [*TV series*]

1973

A Christmas Carol [*Executive producer*]
The Cricket in Times Square [*TV special*]
A Very Merry Cricket [*TV special*]

1974

Yankee Doodle Cricket [*TV special*]
The White Seal [*TV special*]

1975

Rikki-Tikki-Tavi [*TV special*]

1976

Carnival of the Animals [*TV special*]
Mowgli's Brothers [*TV special*]

1978

Bugs Bunny in King Arthur's Court
Raggedy Ann and Andy in: The Great
    Santa Claus Caper

Horton with dust speck:
HORTON HEARS A WHO (1971)

1979

The Bugs Bunny/Road Runner Movie
Daffy Duck's Thanks-for-Giving Special
Bugs Bunny's Looney Christmas Tales
Raggedy Ann and Andy in: The Pumpkin
    Who Couldn't Smile

1980

Bugs Bunny's Bustin' Out All Over
Duck Dodgers and the Return of the
    24½ Century

1983

Heineken commercial

1986

Warner Bros. Golden Jubilee
    [*Animation producer*]

"WATCH HOW THE GRINCH STOLE CHRISTMAS - OR ELSE!"

MAJOR CHARACTERS

☞ Bugs Bunny
✻ Chester Cricket
☞ Claude Cat
✎ Crawford
☞ Daffy Duck
✻ Dot and Line
☞ Elmer Fudd
✎ Gossamer
✻ Grinch
✻ Harry Cat
✎ Henery Hawk

✻ Horton the Elephant
✎ Hugo the Abdominable Snowman
Jerry Mouse
✎ Junyer Bear
✻ Kotick the White Seal
✎ Marc Antony Kitty
✎ Marvin Martian
✻ Mowgli
✻ Milo
✎ Pepé Le Pew
✻ Pogo

☞ Porky Pig
✻ Raggedy Andy
✻ Raggedy Ann
✎ Ralph Wolf
✻ Rikki-Tikki-Tavi
✎ Road Runner
✎ Sam Sheepdog
✎ Sniffles
Tom Cat
✎ Wile E. Coyote
Yosemite Sam

✎ *Character created by Chuck Jones*
☞ *Chuck Jones contributed significantly to character creation and/or development*
✻ *Print media character adapted to animation by Chuck Jones*

EARLY ANIMATION BY CHUCK JONES

1934

The Miller's Daughter
Director: Friz Freleng
Animation: Hamilton, Jones

Those Beautiful Dames
Director: Friz Freleng
Animation: Smith, Jones

1935

Buddy of the Legion
Director: Bugs Hardaway
Animation: Clampett, Jones

My Green Fedora
Director: Friz Freleng
Animation: Clampett, Jones

Buddy Steps Out
Director: Jack King
Animation: Jones, Clampett

Hollywood Capers
Director: Jack King
Animation: Jones, Hamilton

1936

Gold-Diggers of '49
Director: Tex Avery
Animation: Jones, Clampett

The Blow Out
Director: Tex Avery
Animation: Jones, Sutherland

I Love to Singa
Director: Tex Avery
Animation: Jones, Ross

Milk and Money
Director: Tex Avery
Animation: Jones, Ross

1937

Porky the Wrestler
Director: Tex Avery
Animation: Jones, Wait

Picador Porky
Director: Tex Avery
Animation: Jones, Sutherland

Ain't We Got Fun
Director: Tex Avery
Animation: Jones, Clampett